A FARMHOUSE
IN PROVENCE

A FARMHOUSE IN PROVENCE

MARY ROBLEE HENRY

toExcel
San Jose New York Lincoln Shanghai

A Farmhouse in Provence

This edition published by toExcel Press,
an imprint of iUniverse.com, Inc.

For information address:
iUniverse.com, Inc.
620 North 48th Street
Suite 201
Lincoln, NE 68504-3467
www.iuniverse.com

ISBN: 0-595-09165-2

Author's Note

This book is being reprinted at the request of many readers. Also, in the hope that many more readers will share in this cross-cultural quest of an American woman who, with her French husband, discovered and restored an ancient ruin that became their farmhouse in Provence. Now a new generation of vintners thrives and prospers in Séguret, our village in Vaucluse. Modern technology has replaced many of the traditional ways. Property prices have risen. Ruins can no longer be bought for a song, nor a bottle of good wine for a dollar. Still the basic values remain. Roman France, far from the tourist trade of Paris and the Riviera, guards its seductive character, its sunlit stones, its delicious quality of life. In the drama that is Provence, the cast of players may change, but the stage-set remains the same. Or as the French say: Plus ça change, plus c'est la même chose.

For
Paul-Marc
who gave me
France
and for
Roger
who gave us
Provence

. . . kingdom of the sun
edged as with silver braid
by the dazzling Rhône . . .
fantastic faery kingdom of Provence
whose very name casts a magic spell . . .

[FRÉDÉRIC MISTRAL]

Contents

INTRODUCTION xiii

I THE VAUCLUSE: INSTANT LOVE 3

II THE ADVENTURE 16

III GOD'S PLAIN 26

IV POSSESSION OF A PILE OF STONES 43

V BONDS OF FRIENDSHIP 50

VI BUILDING THE ARK 65

VII CASTLE OF SAND? 77

VIII COLD CHRISTMAS IN PROVENCE 90

IX EXPLOSION OF A MYTH 103

X A VINEYARD FOR LA SÉRAFINE 110

XI PAGANS, POPES, AND POETS 120

XII MAÎTRESSE DE MAISON 141

XIII FRIENDS AND NEIGHBORS 156

XIV 6,000 BOTTLES OF WINE 180

XV LOVE AND A VINEYARD 190

Introduction

This is the story of La Sérafine, a pile of stones that became our farmhouse in Provence.

It is the story, too, of a place and the people who live there, of Séguret, a craggy hill town in the Vaucluse, and of the villagers and masons and builders and vintners who helped us to breathe new life into a dying hillside in southern France; Robert Charrasse, our dark-eyed, dashing entrepreneur, and his incredibly efficient squad of Spanish workers; Monsieur Bonell, our wily, balding plumber and electrician; Gilec Aymard, our red-haired master carpenter with the temperament of an artist; the Faravels, who offered us the abundant warmth of their house and became the guardian angels of La Sérafine; Mayor Laurent, who ran on the Communist ticket and was re-elected regularly by the seven hundred and twenty-five citizens of Séguret; the Gaullist postman, who delivered village gossip along with his letters; the family Verdeau, to whom we owe the bushels of cherries and peaches and apricots and plums that fall from our ripened fruit trees; Verdeau father and Verdeau son, whose years of planting and spraying and pruning our vines brought us the unique joy of gathering our own grapes and producing our first heady wine.

In a way, I am a symbol, a reflection of our vineyards—of those Grenache plantings first seeded in French soil centuries ago, then brought across the sea to flourish in America, and of the sturdy American rootstocks later returned to generate new life into the vinelands of France. Norman blood courses

through my veins and my nature echoes the blend of impul-
siveness and adventure which spurred the seafaring ancestors
of my father to forsake the plenty of Normandy for the perils
of New France. Ironically, it was not my father, but my
mother, descended from the British colonizers of Virginia,
who first gave me France. Two indelible years of my childhood were spent touring Europe in the summers and being
schooled by nuns during the winters. Behind the grilled windows of a convent overlooking the Mediterranean my sister
and I sat in blue serge uniforms and learned the subjunctive
and the past imperfect of French grammar, did our *dictée*,
and said our Ave Maria morning and evening in the school
chapel. For half an hour after each silent meal, we were allowed out of the dark halls into the garden for recreation. On
Thursday afternoons, a young nun took her students out, leading us as we walked two by two around the high ramparts of
the village from where we could look down and see the blue,
sun-flecked sea below. When Mother returned from her visits
to London or Paris, we would meet her on the terrace of our
villa and complain about the convent, about the unbending
discipline and the miserable food.

After we went back to America, however, we thought of the
convent with a curious yearning, remembering not the charred
horse meat, but the goblet of watered wine we drank with it;
not the stern, sepulchral face of the Mère Supérieure, but
pretty Sister Marie-Claude letting us play double solitaire
rather than learn the *Fables* of La Fontaine. It was not until
years later that I realized the importance of this small link in
the chain of my destiny, not until I married a Frenchman and
came to live in France and was continually reminded that one
is never alien to a country in which one has been a child.

Introduction

To marry a man is to marry his country. For all their intellectual objectivity, their acceptance of differences, men, more than women, are cast in the armature of nationality. Primordial, instinctive, a woman adapts, recognizes a sameness of condition, seeds in fresh soil.

So, this is the story, too, of striking roots: of an American woman transplanted by marriage to a new ecology—to French family and French friends, French food and French customs, French language and French politics. By the same token, my husband accepted America. Together we have come to understand the varying degrees of sunlight and darkness, and the passage of seasons that revealed the rhythms, cycles, and clocks of each other's cultures.

We stand with a foot on either continent, but we struck root in Provence, with a farmhouse and a vineyard.

In the planting and growing and harvesting of any vineyard, the *cru* varies. Some years are bad, some fair, some excellent. It was the same with La Sérafine. "Thou canst not stir a flower without troubling a star," and if at times we had a crossing of French and American stars, the firmament shone brighter in the end.

In this grafting of differing cultures, I hope that no one appears quaint or ridiculous and that certain undeniable national traits do not become distorted in the mirror of memory. I am thinking, for instance, of the peaks of enthusiasm and the depths of despair, both of which are expressed in the superlatives that so exhaust others with Americans, or the disturbing French tendency to probe hidden levels of reasoning. For us, the lack of practicality often inherent in the French rationale may seem baffling, and the well-turned phrase a mockery of fact, but I hoped to be more than a simple-minded

American coping with the complications of French Cartesian logic, and I wanted to narrow the widening gap. I feel that we did and, in time, became an integral part of the people of Provence.

The difference between Paris and Provence is a wide bridge to span—wider perhaps, than the ocean separating France and America. My husband and I were city people, and cities all over the world incite the same fevers of action and impatience. To the Provençaux we were foreigners, invaders in the guise of conquerors, in their eyes corrupters bringing a potential for change, for good or for evil. It was a moot question. We were the sun-hungry city people; they were the people born to the sun.

The Provençaux are part of their earth, as deeply rooted as the wide-leafed plane trees that shade the village squares and sing with the rubbed-leg cry of cicadas. When they work, they work hard. When they relax, they sit around a metal table at a café in the square and watch a game of *boule* and drink a glass of *pastis* and talk about Provence, about *nous, les Provençaux*. When they talk about *ils*, they mean Paris and the others: the *ils* of the administration against the farmers, the *ils* who maintain the low price of the grapes while the cost of a bottle of wine goes up. In a rural community, such as Séguret, the people may vote Socialist or Communist or Gaullist, but basically they are one. United against *ils*, the others. They close their doors to strangers as they close them to the beating summer sun and to the ravaging mistral wind of winter.

But if the Provençal guards the inherent toughness of the Roman Provincia Romana, he merges it with the sweetest of the French *douceur de vivre*. The Provençaux love Provence. All they ask is for others to share their boundless passion and unswerving conviction that Provence is the most beautiful, the most blessed, and the most bountiful part of the world. Once they are convinced that your heart is there, doors open, the *gigot* is carved, the wine poured, and Provence with all its wit and wisdom and warmth unfurls like a fan.

In breaking down walls and building up walls, we departed from a firm foundation of friendship. The distilled sun-filtered swag of Vaucluse where we settled was first presented to us by friends, Roger and Régine Fabre. It was because they invited us to visit at their big Provence town house and showed us their old hilltop farm that we were inspired to plunge into the arduous, exasperating, exhilarating, and rewarding adventure of restoring Le Sérafine. Little did we realize that the beginning would span five years to the end. Years to see the fruit trees flowering, the vine tendrils pushing up, the empty rooms filling up with solid Provençal armoires and tables. To be accepted by the people of Provence we had to become part of their world, to join the wine cooperative and mix in the squabbles of bottling and labeling, and to contribute to the new look of prosperity in the land.

We brought an unexpected and fresh internationalism to Séguret with our families and friends pouring in from all over the world, and our families and friends found a treasure of peace and beauty in Séguret. Now our *bonne table* is shared by our vintner and my husband's colleagues at the United Nations. French children are speaking English; American children, speaking French. And on summer nights we all sit at a café in the village square and watch a game of *boule* under the plane trees.

Now when I walk under the plum trees near the pool and look up at the rugged white house on the hill, I feel a surge of wonder remembering La Sérafine the first summer day when I found it behind walls of thickets and thornbush. Certainly the most abandoned, unpromising shambles of a property in all Vaucluse, it stank like a festering weed in a gardened world. All around its periphery of twelve acres flowered vineyards and orchards, so carefully planted as to have been embroidered in the soil. But here the olive trees were blighted; the vines had not produced a drinkable goblet of wine in years. The gold-tiled roof lay open to the sky inviting the winter snows and the rains of spring.

We learned later that our patch of the Vaucluse had not always been so humble. As part of the Comtat Venaissin, Séguret fell to the Holy See in 1274, and while the French popes ruled in Avignon for a hundred years the fertile fields around our village thrived. In 1403, the popes returned to Rome, but Avignon and the Comtat Venaissin remained a papal stronghold until the French Revolution. It was then that the Domaine des Michelons, as La Sérafine was originally known, changed hands from the Church to the citizenry. The squat dwelling that housed the bishop's pawn was enlarged by the citizen-peasants to a stony Provençal farmhouse, or *mas*. Goat stalls, a stable, rabbit warrens, and dovecotes were added by their sons and their sons' sons until the house grew into a muscular fortress walled around a courtyard. Green-gold vines lay on the brawny land, olive groves silvered the slopes, and, far below, God's Plain stretched to an infinity of shimmering hills.

Even the remotest flight of fantasy could not have spun such a Vergilian image from the heap of rubble that met my eyes that first fateful day in June. But I was not looking with my eyes. I was seeking with my heart and I loved La Sérafine at once, as one loves a flaking temple. In one afternoon we decided to buy all twelve acres of snarled hillside and crumbling stone, of sun and wind, and a view for the angels.

And there begins the story of our ark.

> . . . *on ne voit bien qu'avec le coeur.*
> *L'essentiel est invisible pour les yeux.*

> [ANTOINE DE SAINT-EXUPÉRY, *Le Petit Prince*]

A FARMHOUSE
IN PROVENCE

THE VAUCLUSE:
INSTANT LOVE

Who travels for love
finds a thousand miles
not longer than one.

[JAPANESE PROVERB]

"You can have it for a *bouchée de pain.*"

Handing me the faded photograph, the notary leaned over his Provençal desk, his spare, dark figure framed against long, half-shuttered windows. Arrows of sunlight stabbed the shadows, striking white walls, black-framed diplomas, law books in Louis Philippe cabinets, and serviceable leather chairs, on one of which I sat, uncomfortably low.

"It's a pile of stones, madame, a ruin. There are other places for sale, town houses and châteaux, but this is the only *mas.*" He pronounced it in the flat Midi "a"—"maaa."

3

"We want a farmhouse, Monsieur le Notaire, not a châ-teau." A young man in black cotton cuff shields slid in over the waxed tiles with a sheaf of papers, eying me through his green visor before sliding out, banging the tall doors as if to peal the noon hour.

"Another person has the deed. He will take you to see it," said the notary, ringing the operator of Vaison-la-Romaine.

"The Balkan painter in Old Vaison, please. 'Allo. 'Allo, can you take Madame, une Américaine, to visit the farm-house in Séguret? Yes. Madame is staying where?" He turned to me.

"At the house of Roger Fabre."

"The Fabre house, Quai Pasteur, at seventeen hours."

The name Fabre, I noticed, produced a furrow of surprise on the dehydrated brow of Monsieur le Notaire.

"Let me know what you think of the little place," he said, leading me through a tangle of parched lavender and bruised geraniums to the tall wrought-iron gates.

Noon in Vaison-la-Romaine. I walked up the narrow Grand' Rue lined with shops, past Hadrian's blanched half-dug heap, to the string of cafés spread under green branches on the Place de Montfort.

"Un coup de blanc," I ordered at the Café du Commerce and propped the snapshot against the parasol shaft for a long look at the farmhouse. Encircling a courtyard, it was a mini-ature fortress of fat walls, flaked, warmed by foliage. A few shutters swung on loose hinges from eyeless holes. Lots of roofs with wavy tiles dipped down, leaning on green-shoul-dered hillocks. The house looked alone and lost, but it seemed firmly planted and grown in its own earth, a stone flower awaiting the honeybees.

The Vaucluse: Instant Love

I must show it to Roger and Régine, I thought, with sudden panic at the hour. At the Fabre house meals were served on time and guests were not expected to abuse the usual French *quart d'heure de grâce* that might mean the collapse of a steamy soufflé.

Any minute now the cafés would be filling up for the noonday *pastis*. Iron grilles would be rattled down over shopwindows, vegetable stalls buried under canvas, doors bolted behind yellow and red plastic streamers. Beetle-quick cars and bicycles, trucks and buses would be squeezing over the cat-backed span of the Ouvèze River. Peppery-eyed girls, masons in blue work clothes, the Curé, his cassock billowing from his Vespa, children out of school—everyone would be rushing home for lunch carrying a long loaf of bread. Into dark-tiled rooms with the gold air blanked out, they would sit down at the family table, at their places marked with wooden napkin rings and with forks laid tines-down. For two hours Vaison would die, the hot silence broken only by the call of cicadas in the high green reaches of plane trees.

With a pang, I realized that Régine Fabre would never be caught the way I was, dawdling bare-legged in a street café with lunch ready and waiting on the table. She would not, in fact, be caught dawdling at a café alone in Vaison at any time. Just the night before, after Roger had gone to bed early, I had asked Régine to walk to the square with me for a drink in the café, to see the lively fair that whirled around the esplanade overlooking the Roman ruins, but she had explained very discreetly that she could not. In the provinces, it was not done. Wives didn't go to cafés at night without their husbands, and especially not Madame Roger Fabre, the wife of the leading industrialist of Vaison-la-Romaine. Everyone

5

would be gossiping and criticizing and wondering what had got into the dignified young Madame Fabre, who, though not from Provence, had adapted so perfectly to the customs of the country. In the afternoon, it was correct and admirable for her to take the children to ride on the ferris wheel and have a *goûter* at the fair. As a foreigner, I could stroll through the streets day or night and sip wine alone at any one of the hundred tables of the five cafés that made the square seem a huge outdoor salon. The people would be amused to see an American, dazed and delighted by the carnival that brought a sudden surge of life to their sleepy little town. But whereas I was a stranger, Madame Fabre was by marriage *du pays* and, as such, expected to conform to the rules of the *noblesse oblige* to which she belonged.

In a way, I was a stranger to the Fabres too, and for the first time feeling my way alone in the complex labyrinth of French family life without the support of my French husband, Paul-Marc. Unlike Americans who love to entertain foreigners, displaying them like captured trophies to their friends and families, the French guard the privacy of the home for immediate members of the clan, and for the tribe of their aunts, uncles, and cousins. Outsiders rarely penetrate further than the formal salon or the dining room. Far less reserved than most French families, the Fabres were exceptionally international and hospitable and had been close friends of my husband for years, ever since they had been on diplomatic post together in Lebanon. We had often dined at each other's houses in Paris; and, rather than reserve, Régine had shown a charming persistence in inviting us to visit in Provence on our way back from Morocco, where I had accompanied my husband on a brief diplomatic mission. Although we had

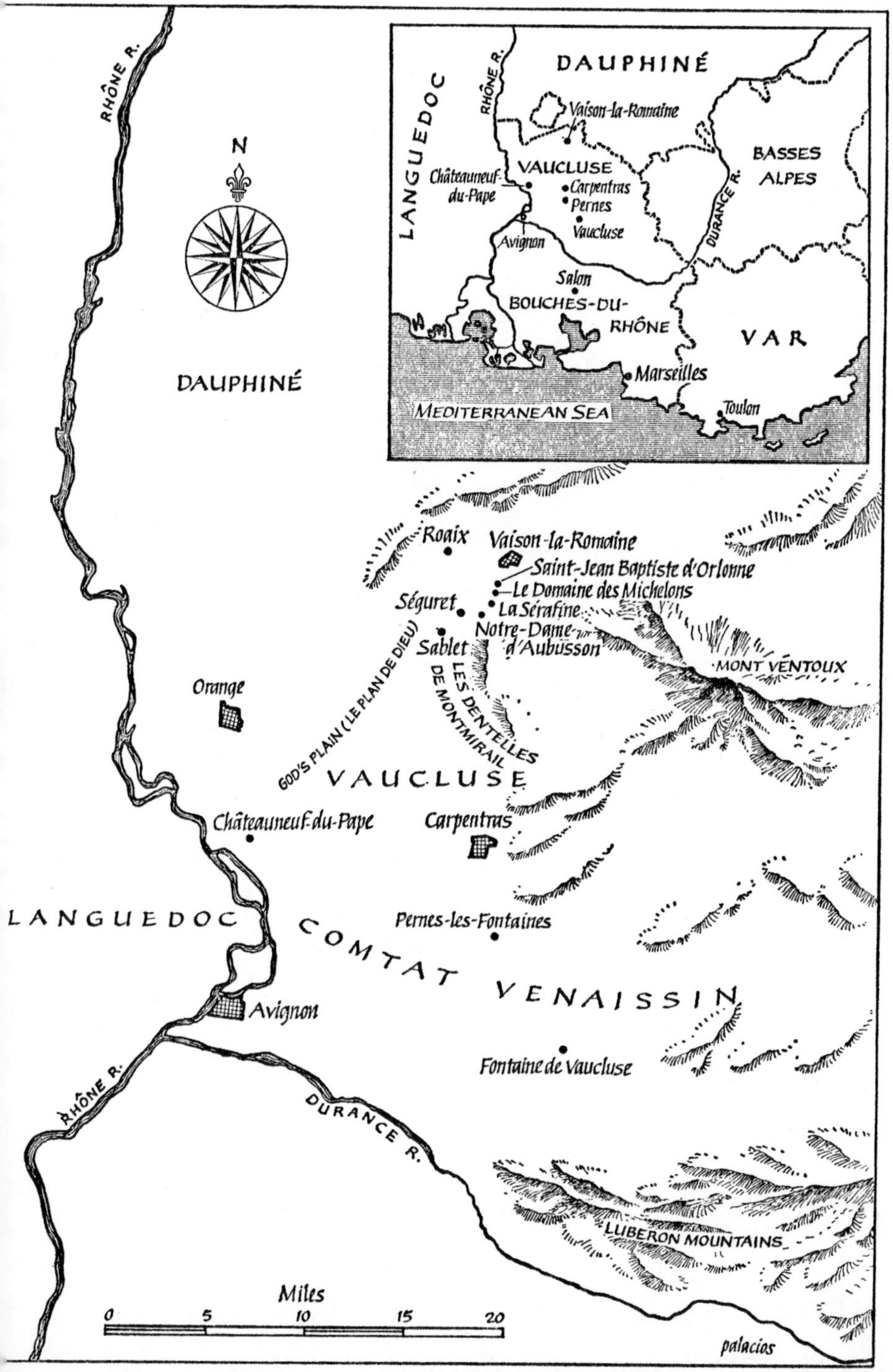

DAUPHINÉ
LANGUEDOC
RHÔNE R.
Vaison-la-Romaine
VAUCLUSE
Châteauneuf-du-Pape
Carpentras
Pernes
Vaucluse
Avignon
BASSES ALPES
DURANCE R.
Salon
BOUCHES-DU-RHÔNE
VAR
Marseilles
Toulon
MEDITERRANEAN SEA
N
RHÔNE R.
DAUPHINÉ
Roaix
Vaison-la-Romaine
Saint-Jean Baptiste d'Orlonne
Le Domaine des Michelons
Séguret
La Sérafine
Notre-Dame-d'Aubusson
Sablet
MONT VENTOUX
Orange
GOD'S PLAIN (LE PLAN DE DIEU)
LES DENTELLES DE MONTMIRAIL
VAUCLUSE
Châteauneuf-du-Pape
Carpentras
LANGUEDOC
Pernes-les-Fontaines
COMTAT VENAISSIN
Avignon
Fontaine de Vaucluse
RHÔNE R.
DURANCE R.
LUBERON MOUNTAINS
Miles
0
5
10
15
20
palacios

skimmed through Provence on the way to the Riviera, neither of us had ever been to the town of Vaison-la-Romaine, nor were we particularly anxious to go at that time. But as the plane between Rabat and Paris stopped in Marseilles, we accepted the Fabres' invitation for a weekend.

Régine had cabled that Marcel, the chauffeur, would meet us at the airport with a black Peugeot and take us to their house deep in the *département* of the Vaucluse. Round, jolly, shaggy-haired, and deaf to klaxons, Marcel had driven us by fields of yellow sesame, through tunnels of plane trees, past golden villages, up curling hills and down into sun-blazed valleys at such breakneck speed that the landscape fragmented before our eyes like a gigantic jigsaw of a Van Gogh canvas. By the time we arrived at the Fabre town house we were dizzy but delighted that Régine had insisted on our coming.

All weekend the Fabres had shown us the countryside, fresh and shining in a June glaze. They took us to see Chanteduc, the place on the crest of a hill they had just bought, a peasant's farmhouse, called a *mas* in Provence. One look at its weathered stones and minuscule rooms had cast a spell. When Régine suggested I spend the week and let Paul-Marc come back for me the following weekend, I accepted. I took one more look at the faded photograph given me by the notary. Had I found a *mas* for us in Provence? Church bells were ringing. The sacred hour, the midday dinner bell.

I paid my franc for the wine and rushed down rue Jean Jaurès to the Quai Pasteur bordering the river. A group of old men, their bland faces rosy with wine under their dark berets, rolled and pointed their lead balls in an endless game of *boule*. At the end of a shaded lane stood the Fabre house, La Maison

Fabre, pale-yellow stucco, its sequence of blue shutters tight, its bulk fastened to the street. No doubt the notary would like to interest me in a bourgeois house like this one, I thought, something of high value and pale character. A monument to respectability built in the nineteenth century, the house had been inherited by Roger Fabre along with the family business from his father, a senator from the Vaucluse who had been deeply loved and revered by his constituents. Roger had not followed his father into politics but had left the Foreign Service to run the Fabre firm of agricultural machinery, dividing his time between Paris and Vaison-la-Romaine. For him, this staid house held all the remembrances of a happy childhood, and Régine had preserved the traditional atmosphere for their three young sons, Renaud, Guilhem, and Jean-Charles. And in the traditional manner, the entire family would probably be seated around the lunch table by now.

I quailed as I tapped the brass knocker of the polished walnut door, but fortunately the boys came tumbling down the red-carpeted stairs as I was let into the dark cool hall.

"Hello, shall we have an apéritif before lunch?" said Roger Fabre, looking tall, loose-limbed, and elegant, as he emerged from his study and kissed my hand before opening the doors to the living room. The boys switched on lamps and sat stiffly, their brown knees shining, in gilt Louis-Quinze chairs. On the marble coffee table, a silver tray held Perrier water, a bucket of ice, and Rasteau, the sweetly cloying wine of the country, which we had in crystal goblets.

"My dear Roger, it is already twelve forty-five," said Régine Fabre, much too well brought up to reproach me for my tardiness. Cleopatra of the Périgord. Régine was well named; her green eyes flashed and her dark hair, fringed across the brow, swung straight down on strong tanned shoulders. Born a baroness, she had been raised in a gloomy vaulted château in a green country full of ghosts and fortress churches. The lucid red and gold of Provence had never completely seduced her. But Roger was a man rooted in the Midi, and Régine, the perfect *maîtresse de maison*, ran her bourgeois house as a châtelaine her castle. You could hear her keys clanking from her waist as she strode down the hall to open the linen room for soap or towels or special silver wrapped in flannel. All eyes were upon the beautiful Madame Fabre on her market rounds early Tuesday mornings, when the food was fresh and new in the open-air stalls of Vaison. Her cook followed her, and pinching, smelling, hovering over every leaf of spinach, they would pile up their baskets and stock the larder with all the best pâtés, spring lambs, black olives, fruits, and goats' cheeses of the Vaucluse. Small wonder that every meal at the Fabre house was a masterwork.

"Madame est servie," said the maid sliding back the dining-room doors to a long table dazzling under a crystal chandelier. Chinks of sunlight filtered through the barred windows, which I longed to fling open to the dry reviving air. But this was the South of France, *Le Midi*, the noon country where the suspect sun is the lover of the wine grape which it blazes, caresses to bursting gold. The same sun that withers man, blinds, fades, fatigues with demanding brilliance. When the sun bedded down in its orange and silver blankets, the windows would be opened to the river and the firefly lights of Old Vaison flickering on up the hill.

After the wine had been poured, the three boys told to keep their wrists on the table, and the rolls unfolded from our napkins, Régine said in her sweet uptilted voice, "I have a surprise. Your husband called from Paris while you were out. He will arrive tonight for the weekend."

"What luck. Then we can look at the property together."
I pulled out the yellowed photograph and showed it to Régine. "I have an appointment to see it this afternoon. Where
is the village of Séguret?"

"In the Countship, too, just a few miles south," said Roger,
referring to the Comtat Venaissin, that part of the Vaucluse
that for five hundred years had belonged to the Vatican.

"It is a real *mas*, but a ruin. But why a place here . . .
why not the Blue Coast, the Silver Coast, the sea?" Régine
spent as much time in Paris as she did in Provence, and in August sent the boys to the wild wet coast of Brittany for a change
of air.

"How nice that an American would want to be near us in
the Vaucluse," said Roger, whose father, Senator Ulysse
Fabre, had helped win an official *appellation contrôlée* of the
Côtes-du-Rhône for the Countship wines. The molten grape
minted red-gold in the pockets of peasant vintners. Cooperatives sprang up like weeds. The name Fabre became magic
in the Countship as the wines of Caesar and the popes flowed
throughout France, throughout the world. But for all the
Senator's work for the local wine economy, the Fabres had
been landless industrialists, residents of this big town house
with not a vineyard to their names until Régine had found
Chanteduc, their vine-wrapped farmhouse in the shadow of
Mont Ventoux.

"Of course it would be sensational if you could find a place
like Chanteduc. I must go up this afternoon and see what's
happening with the new grapes." To Régine, Chanteduc was
her *petit hameau*, her very own plaything. The big old
town house was somber with memory, ridden with past glory.
Maman Fabre's bedroom, for instance, remained enshrined

behind sealed doors, unlocked only every Thursday to spittle and polish her silver hairbrushes, dust her treasures, preserve her sanctuary as she had departed from it, from her deathbed. The *belle-mère* would always reign as phantom queen in this house. Régine was merely the dauphine. But Chanteduc was different; there she was Marie Antoinette with a toy house and a yielding vineyard.

Until I had seen the squat little heaven that was Chanteduc I had never longed for a house in the country. The thought of settling down in one place seemed death in the soul to me. My childhood had been fairly nomadic and my adult life had been spent shifting from continent to continent in a whirlwind of change. Even my own work involved moving about, and it was in just such a moment of continental whirlwind that destiny led me to a new life in France.

As travel editor of a fashion magazine in New York, I had been asked to cover the first transatlantic jet flight from New York to Paris and back. It happened at the last minute. Two days in flight, two nights in Paris. I barely had time to pack, much less answer a call from a friend asking me to deliver a message to a diplomat at the French Ministry of Foreign Affairs. I noted the number in my address book and forgot it. Flicking through the pages in Paris, I came across the name again and, conscience-stricken, called. Perhaps because of my inexpert French, the unseen diplomat at the other end of the line got the impression that I was not from *l'Amérique*, but a missionary on my way to *l'Afrique*. As a specialist in African affairs, he felt in honor bound to see me. It was a dreary prospect, but with punctilious *politesse* and as a friend of a friend, he offered to stop by my hotel on his way home. I had been invited to a dinner party so I dressed early and went down to the lobby to wait, watching the revolving doors for the entrance of a likely French diplomat. I pictured him with a rosette of the Legion of Honor on his lapel, probably an older man, very suave and dignified. The minutes ticked by. There was no message at the desk so I began writing a sorry-to-have-missed-you note. Just then a broad-shouldered man with fierce brown eyes and a head of shaggy black curls charged to the desk. "Vous-êtes l'amie de . . . but you don't look like a missionary!" Nine flights across the Atlantic and three months later we were married.

For a year and a half we had lived in Paris, not settling in too much there as we knew that eventually a new post would come along. It could be anywhere—Africa, Asia, Latin America, and we both loved this unknown quantity of diplomatic life. When Paul-Marc traveled to conferences, I often went with him, collecting material for articles which I wrote in the quiet of our garden apartment. Even there I missed the clatter and conversation of my colleagues at the magazine in New York. If at times I felt lonesome for my American friends in Paris, how would I feel in the remote reaches of Provence?

On the other hand, these rare moments of alienation in a strange land might disappear with the sense of belonging that springs from putting down roots. I had married a Frenchman and no matter how far and wide we traveled, our home would be France. A house that we could build up together would be a bond to our marriage and, for me, a fixed symbol of identity with France, my second country. We needed a nucleus to the periphery of our lives, one small mound of earth on which to create a microcosm, not only for ourselves but for our families. Most especially, it would strengthen my link with Paul-Marc's children by his former marriage, Jacques and Nicole. For them it would be a place to be *en famille* with us and, when we were abroad, a place to bring their friends. If only we could find another Chanteduc. What a surprise for Paul-Marc if during the week he had been in Paris, I had discovered a plot for us in Provence. I could barely contain my eagerness to see the farmhouse in Séguret.

THE ADVENTURE

—*green reeds, vines, ivy, fig trees,*
olives, pomegranates with lusty flowers
of the brightest orange;
hundred-year-old cypresses,
half-broken flights of steps,
ogive windows in ruins.

[VAN GOGH]

At five sharp, a white Simca drove up, top down. The Balkan painter alighted, a slight man with small blue eyes and spiky blond hair to his nape. As we sped down the road, sun-freckled, bowered in plane trees, he told me that he had stayed on in Vaison after the war, fixing a house in the old town as a studio. Bit by bit he had acquired a few properties but wanted to sell this one as, frankly, he hadn't the time to restore it.

Of course the place needed some redoing; it had been deserted since the death of the old farmer who had lived there. An acre of land surrounded the house, enough for a vineyard and an olive grove. He had just sold a larger house with more land just above this one to a German woman, the curator of a museum. Only sun-hungry northerners and city-trapped people wanted Provençal places. Naturally he had several other buyers clamoring for this farm, one of the few for sale in the region.

The price? A *bouchée de pain*—a chunk of bread. He would ask more in francs, but for dollars he would settle for five thousand. Cash.

The breeze blew pungent whiffs of pine and lavender as we hurtled by walls of cypresses and rows of sunflowers bobbing their shaggy blond heads. Solid stone houses stood becalmed, their seas of vines rippled by orange tractors put-putting through the swell. Beyond the racing foothills, an edge of white peaks cut the blank blue sky. On the graveled river bed, troupes of gypsies camped, their pretty, beady-eyed children stuffing stolen cherries into their mouths, spitting the pits at passing cars. Road signs pointed to Carpentras, Orange, Avignon.

The name Carpentras meant nothing to me at the time, but Avignon and Orange evoked disturbing memories of motoring through this world five years ago, long before the vagaries of love and destiny had brought me back to France. How strange to feel instant recognition for a landscape now that once had appeared hostile, impenetrable, even sinister. The light had been as brilliant, the air as soft, the sky as blue as it was today; but then the Route of the Princes of Orange was just a line on a road map, a snarl in flight between Rome and London. The black-fingered cypresses, now spires of hope, had then seemed symbols of death. Marches of vine-yards around the rib cages of hilltowns struck topaz by the sun had looked bony and bereft. Crazed by heat and noise, I had spun around the cheese-white walls of Avignon barely glancing at the towering Rock of the Lord and Bénézet's Bridge, jutting like a broken arm into the murky depths of the river Rhône.

At Orange, a low-keyed mistral wind whipped stagnant canals, raising a vaporous stench through thin gray streets of faceless houses. A random inn, with rush-seated chairs and red Provençal hangings in the hall, had spiders in the bed-room and brown linoleum under a naked bidet, an atmos-phere so dismal that I had left at dawn, snaking behind col-umns of cars; their wheels which throbbed on cobbles seemed a thousand-legged monster thrashing, hissing through villages from which the villagers had fled.

Had I listened I might have heard the music of Provence, the morning cries of the marketplace, the drip of a moss-bearded fountain, the silence of noon cut by the clank of cut-lery behind barred shutters. Had I looked, I might have seen the Caesarian bones of temples filtered by the distilled light of Petrarch's Closed Valley. But that was five years too soon. Then I was racing home to America, bewitched by the jew-eled eyes of Italy, blinded to Roman France.

Suddenly, I was jolted out of my reveries as we veered into the hills. Sinuous, so tight that the tires tore the yellow broom along its banks, the lane led upward, past a mound of acreage with a baroque chapel set in pines. Shifting gears, we skidded over a hump of bridge, by barking dogs and high grilled gates screening a pale house. Finally, blocked by trees and a stretch of vineland, we ground to a halt.

The Adventure

"Le premier pas est toujours le plus difficile," said the painter as we waded through powdery furrows, waist-high in tendrils curled over chignons of agate grapes. Part of the property, I assumed, until we began climbing into thickets and dwarf maples. Prickly branches tore my pants and bloodied my ankles as we beat a path through the bush, loud with bumblebees and crickets. Crackling underfoot, the scent of sun-cooked herbs assaulted the senses. We pushed on, higher and higher, deeper and deeper into the hills.

There is no house, he's putting me on, I began to think when we came upon a row of ratty cypresses curving toward a whey-colored façade of shuttered windows and a barricaded door veiled in cobwebs. The sloping roof was orange and seemed oddly new. This, I was told, was the new "pavilion"; but we would have to enter on the eighteenth-century side, by way of the north gray wall. The high wooden portals set in pillars under a tiled roof refused to yield. Kicking, pushing, straining, the owner sprang the lock.

In the courtyard we were blocked by a wall of thornbrush coiling over terraces, up the walls, and into the half-opened entrance. Picking up a rusty hoe, the owner hacked a swath to the door.

Inside the house seemed incredibly dank and dark. What great beast might pounce from this black cave, I wondered scanning the room, but found only a frieze of perfect shiny scorpions on the flaked walls. In one corner a shallow granite sink stood beside a crumbling chimneypiece; arched doorways led to a dripping cistern, an olive press, a vast stable stacked with rotten beams. A pair of broken stone staircases triangled the room reaching to the upper story. Over our heads the ceiling belled like an upside-down cupola.

"All this is easily restored," the owner said, noticing my crestfallen face. "The point is the original plan. Perfect. Come upstairs and have a look."

Breaching the slippery steps, as rounded and smooth as the overkissed toe of Peter, I peered into a sagging loft. This could be a bedroom, I thought, probably because of the mildewed mattress lying lumpily among wisps of hay. In another room a rip in the roof let in hot rays of sun which fell on a rusted motorbike and a pair of old army boots.

"The maquisards hid out here during the war. I remember all that," said the owner, implying that he might have been one of them.

As we eased down the narrow steps, ducking our heads to avoid the low stone lintels, a whir, a flapping and squeaking cut the damp air. I felt the hard-webbed slap of a bat's wing against my hair. Taking the steps two by two I fled into the sunlight as the flying rats swooped by me into the little house in the courtyard.

My stone flower is a stinkweed, I thought, chilled with terror.

"You must see the little house," the owner said.

"With those bats in there, never," I protested. "Anyway, my husband would have to see the place. In France, Frenchmen make the decisions."

The painter laughed at my panic, twinkling his ice-blue eyes as he closed the portals, assuring me that bats always nest in abandoned houses and this place had been empty for years. Too many years, I thought, thoroughly disenchanted with my discovery. Only the lime tree shading a crumbling wall looked healthy and beautiful and alive, making a mockery of this mournful hovel. And then, framed in a branch of lime blossoms, it exploded before my eyes—the view. All the splendor of Provence mapped in the valley below. I stood at the apex of an amphitheater, winged on one side by a knoll of pineland, on the other by an amber peasant house couched in the lap of a hill. And fanning out to a horizon of ocher cliffs lay God's Plain, its infinity of vineyards serene and silent under a vault of yellow sun. I was spellbound. All of a sudden I could imagine this forsaken aerie gloriously re-created as a garden of earthly delights.

As we tracked back down the matted hillside my eyes kept turning, magnetized, to the shimmering plain below. Until he said, "You are trespassing on private property," I didn't see the man blocking our path, his gun cracked over his arm.

❦

"I was sure he was going to kill us," I said that night as we sat on the terrace having coffee and cognac after dinner. My husband had arrived from Paris and I had been telling him and the Fabres of my strange experience with the painter and the menacing appearance of the unknown assailant.

"Too much American zeal. You should have waited for your French husband," said Paul-Marc, who found my adventure enormously funny.

"You say he was stocky with dark hair," said Roger.

"Yes, and he had a vicious little brown dog that snapped at us, something like a corgi, but I don't think it was a corgi."

"It must have been Monsieur Faravel with his truffle dog. He was probably out hunting truffles and songbirds for his pâté," said Régine, adding that the reason for the silent, songless air of Vaucluse was the Provençal passion for pâté of thrush.

"Of course he has guns," Roger said. "Faravel used to be with the Paris police force. And everyone here loves to hunt —hare, birds, truffles, mushrooms, everything. But it isn't the season, so he was not out hunting."

"He was stalking us. He definitely wanted us to get off the property."

"The mystery may lie with your Balkan painter," said Paul-Marc.

"He is a strange character. No one really knows very much about his past," said Régine, implying that it was a bad one.

"Tomorrow we'll make a little promenade over to see the Faravels and find out what it's all about," said Roger. "That is, of course, if it was Faravel. It may have been Girard, who owns the big manor house with the chapel. He is known to dislike outsiders, but Faravel is a good sort. We've known him for years."

"Il faut se méfier," said Régine, using the constant French admonition to stay on guard.

"People here seem warm and smiling, but underneath they are suspicious of foreigners. To them, Parisians are strangers, to say nothing of Americans or Balkans."

"They have a right to be," said Paul-Marc. "After having been invaded by everyone from the Romans to the Saracens and the Germans, now they have the Parisians and the Americans to fend off."

It could be that, of course, I thought. Perhaps the local people did not welcome the idea of foreigners as landowners in the region. The Balkan painter had mentioned the fact that a German woman had bought the house above and, with my fair looks, the man with the gun may have taken me for another German about to invade his territory. Understandably not a pleasant prospect for him considering that the maquisards had found refuge during the war in the place I had just seen. Obviously I was a stranger in Séguret, and he had no way of knowing that I, as an American married to a Frenchman, felt a natural desire to own property in Provence. The owner said lots of people were anxious to buy the place and if there were such a choice, the farmers might make a point of indicating a hostility to any but local neighbors. It was true, I should have waited for my husband, or perhaps I should have spoken to the strange man instead of dashing for the car like a startled doe. But the painter had seemed as eager as I to flee and had offered no explanation for the interloper, except to pass him off as he had the bats by saying that one always sees odd characters roaming about abandoned properties.

"I haven't heard of any land for sale in Séguret," said Roger. "I'm sure Faravel would have mentioned it to me if it borders his vineyards."

"The notary arranged it all for me. He said it was in Séguret and I saw the road sign pointing that way, but I have no idea whether the man was Monsieur Faravel or not. I have only the word of the Balkan painter to go on," I answered.

"He is considered rather an odd character," Régine said. "He came to Vaison and started a studio for artists after the war."

"It sounds as though you have stumbled into a basket of crabs," Paul-Marc said. "Did you see any papers, did he show you the deed to the property?"

I was beginning to feel foolish, the gullible American taken in by a clever European. As usual I was being overenthusiastic, jumping to conclusions with no sound evidence that the property, such as it was, actually could be bought. I had not embroidered too much on the condition of the house, but raved about the view from the hillside and the fact that the place could be had for a song. But could it be had at all?

Roger, always so kind, realized my uneasiness and reassured me by saying that we would retrace my footsteps the next day and try to disentangle the mystery.

"We will pay a call on Monsieur and Madame Faravel tomorrow and see the lay of the land before making any further moves."

We said good night and Paul-Marc and I groped down the long red-carpeted hall, past *Maman* Fabre's bolted door to our room. Mineral water with glasses and a stack of books had been placed on the lamp tables. White embroidered linen sheets were turned down from ruffled square pillows slanted against a bolster on the big sleigh bed. A massive armoire stood against one wall, and on the marble-topped desk bloomed a bouquet of anemones. Across the hall was the bathroom with its ball-and-clawfoot tub, its chain-pull toilet in a separate cubicle. White towels as large as sheets warmed on the steam pipes.

I finished unpacking Paul-Marc's valise and put his things in the polished chest between the long shuttered windows. Then I pulled the heavy bolster off the bed and folded it onto the pale-green rug. Almost at a leap, each one of us took a window, and slipping the iron bolts swung back the solid-blue doors to let in the winy night air, the nightingale's music. Weeping willows trailed in the rustling river below and Old Vaison flared with the orange flame lighting the derelict fortress on the hill. Beyond lay Chanteduc, whose twin I had hoped to find. The ruin in Séguret was admittedly a poor relation, far more crumbling than the Fabres' little farmhouse. The photograph I had shown Paul-Marc idealized the reality, but I hoped that the view would make up for the dilapidation and he would see the reasons for restoring the house. That was, of course, if it were available at all. I fell asleep full of doubts and awakened with fearful anticipation of his reaction to my discovery. He might very well say, *Il y a des possibilités*, or he might very well say, *Ma chère petite, tu exagères.*

GOD'S PLAIN

Last night I saw in a dream
landscapes with skies all rose . . .

[COROT]

The next afternoon we packed into the sturdy little 2 CV
Citroën and drove through the valley to call on Monsieur and
Madame Faravel. Roger took the long way around to show
Paul-Marc the village of Séguret, which from a distance
seemed to be belted around the waist of a thick mountain.
"It's practically deserted now," Roger said. "Most of the villagers have moved to the plain or to larger towns." Not a
plume of smoke rose from the chimneys of the orange roofs
of houses shuttered against the western sun. Immobile and
silent, the village basked in calm, a honeyed carving against
a wall of endless blue.

"During the time of the Avignon popes, Séguret was al-

ways at sword's point with Sablet over there." Régine pointed
to a neighboring village that lay as still and round as a car-
dinal's hat thrown upon the ground. "Now Sablet is like a
town in Andalusia; all the farm workers who came from
Spain to harvest the grapes live there. At first just the men
came, but because of the higher wages in France they brought
their families and now you hear nothing but Spanish in the
streets."

"Are all these vineyards part of the Côtes-du-Rhône?"
asked Paul-Marc, his keen economist's eye scanning the
carpets of vines spread wall to mountain wall.

"Yes, and the wine cooperative is across the valley. Séguret and Roaix share it," said Régine, pointing to another
village edging a hill on the far side of the valley. "The wine
is twelve to fourteen degrees, very strong, red and *rosé*.
Some of the people are very rich. Monsieur Meffre, for example, he developed all the vineyards on God's Plain, fifteen hundred acres between here and Orange. He owns vineyards in the village of Gigondas and in Châteauneuf-du-Pape
as well. He makes a fortune."

"Yes, but most of the people work their own land," said
Roger. "The Vaucluse is largely rural, with thousands of
farms. Lots of the farmers are *primeurs*, growing produce.
About one hundred thousand tons a year are shipped from
Avignon to Paris and all over Europe. The winegrowers are
very well organized. The grapes are harvested, then trucked
to the cooperatives, where they are weighed, then pressed,
and the wine aged in oaken vats. The vintner is paid by
weight and alcoholic degree." We passed the Roaix-Séguret
cooperative, a big stone block, ugly and new, with its garish
sign "Dégustation" spread across the entrance.

Régine pointed out the Mayor's place. "He owns large

peach orchards and still works his vineyards with a mule. He has been in office since the war when he was elected on the Communist platform."

"I wonder how much he's done for the Commune," said Roger. "We must ask Faravel, who I think is a Radical Socialist, as my father found him a job when Daladier was prime minister."

"It would be interesting to know what Meffre's politics are," said Régine. "He's a kind of American capitalist with his hundreds of hectares of vineyards."

"A very modern type for this region," said Roger. "And of course the small vintners resent his method. He's brought in big American and Italian machinery, tractors and bulldozers, and masses of Spaniards to work the vines and pick the grapes. People here are used to small holdings, family properties that have been passed on from father to son. The wives and daughters help pick the grape harvest and now they hire the Spaniards to lend a hand. Basically, the peasants resent change; they like their traditional ways. But things are changing. In the last few years Meffre has transformed the Plan de Dieu."

"How did it ever come to be called God's Plain? Because it is so blessed?"

"Just the opposite, because it was so diabolical a few hundred years ago," said Roger. "Travelers between Orange and Vaison were so terrified of the road that they had themselves blessed with holy water by the priest in the church of the village of Travaillan. The scrub and trees were crawling with brigands and highwaymen who stopped the horses, raided the carriages, and robbed or held the passengers for ransom. It was called God's Plain simply because you had to put yourself in the hands of God to get through it."

Nowhere in the world could have seemed more peaceful or prosperous than that valley now as we skimmed along the curving road leading to the Faravels. "Ah, here's where we turn," Roger said and swung into the foothills and up the lane bordered in yellow broom. I recognized the road by the small chapel on the hill, a landmark distingushing it from all the other dusty turn-offs we had passed. We bounced up over the bridge and swerved into a driveway flanked by two soaring cypress trees. "Les cyprès d'accueil," Régine explained, "the symbolic tree of welcome in Provence and every farmhouse has at least one at the entrance as a sign of hospitality." I hoped this would be a good omen and that Monsieur Faravel, if the man with the gun had been Monsieur Faravel, would greet me more in the spirit of his cypress trees than in the tradition of the brigands of God's Plain.

We walked down the path to the graveled courtyard, where a willow tree wept its pale-green tears onto a scarred metal table. Sunrays fell like organ pipes over the white stucco house, its aquamarine blinds open to the afternoon breeze. I could see an ebony eye peering from a corner of the window. Then Monsieur Faravel burst through the ribboned door-curtain and bounded down the stone steps, his arms outstretched. "Monsieur Fabre, Madame Fabre. What a joy. That you should pay us a visit. We are enchanted!"

"Dear Faravel, forgive us for coming unannounced, but I wanted my friends from Paris to see your beautiful property." Roger introduced us, making no mention of my visit to the neighboring place the day before. I felt relieved to see that this ebullient, merry-eyed character was the same stern gunman I had seen on the hillside, but, as he greeted me as though he had seen me for the first time, I gave no sign of recognition. It would be unpardonably crass to bring up such an embarrassing encounter, and recognizing the rules of Provençal courtesy, I decided to wait for him to make the first gesture.

Monsieur Faravel pulled metal chairs around the table, talking all the time about how pleased he was to see us, how he would show us his flourishing fields, how his trees had produced a ton of Montmorency cherries, what excellent wine his grapes yielded and how we must have a glass at once. Madame Faravel would be there in a minute to welcome us, and meanwhile he would fetch the wine. His own special *cru,* he assured us, from his own cellars. "The cooperative is all right for table wine, but for my friends I make my own," he said and crunched over the gravel, his bowed hairy legs forming parentheses from his cuffed blue shorts to his leather sandals.

Except for a ribbon of water falling into a shell-shaped font on the wall, silence hung like a dome engulfing us into a bubble world where every shape and creature stood out in acute perspective. Nothing moved except within the courtyard. A nye of pheasant, a few banana-beaked ducks, a mother hen nesting on a mound of eggs the size of ping-pong balls, and a bevy of quail all quacked and clucked and pecked in a wired cage. From the garage that housed the Faravels' small plastic-covered Citroën came sundry growled complaints from the pig-eyed truffle dog as he scratched his stiff brown coat against the deep granite laundry tub. On the far side of the little house in the courtyard, a twirling spray sprinkled rows of marigolds, poppies, and dahlias planted under the leafy arms of a mulberry tree.

"Bonjour," said Madame Faravel as she came toward us, a slender, dark-haired young woman in a printed cotton dress.

She seemed almost too slight to carry the big round tray filled with glasses and dishes of black olives, pâté, and salted crackers. After placing the tray on the table, she shook hands, scanning each one of us with her nervous brown eyes. She was delighted by our visit, but of course it was unexpected. Madame Fabre would understand if everything was not in perfect order, but what could one do with no telephones to be had in Provence. Séguret could hardly be called the most modern part of France.

"Be quiet, Chou-Chou," she called to the truffle dog who had begun to yap with joy at the sound of her pointed Parisian voice.

Monsieur Faravel came up from the cellar with a pair of dusty gray bottles cradled like twin babies in the crooks of his arms. "Mine. Mine," he said uncorking them and pouring the rosy liquid into the glasses. He handed Roger and Paul-Marc each a glass and they whirled the stems until the wine swirled and dripped lees from the lip of the glass. Then they sniffed and made purrings of approval before lifting the rim to their lips. They raised the wine to the light and peered at its gold-shot profile, then took a long sip. Faravel seemed suspended in air, his eyes followed every gesture of the ritual as he waited for the verdict.

"It is sun in a bottle!" said Roger.

"Little Jesus sliding down the throat in satin pants!" said Paul-Marc.

Faravel's face splintered into a pumpkin grin. With the strong brown hands that had planted, picked, and pressed the grapes, he grasped the bottles at the base and filled all the glasses. As the cool young wine stung and soothed our parched throats, Madame Faravel passed the crackers and pâté.

"It is thrush. I make it myself," she said with a bashful smile.

The taste was delicate, velvety, touched with a tang of truffles. "It takes seven birds for one pâté. I hunt them in the woods. And the truffles too, our famous black pearls of Provence. Chou-Chou, our little dog over there, ferrets them out with his nose. He's a crack," said Monsieur Faravel passing the crinkled black olives and explaining that they too came from his grove and Madame spiked them with a fork before preserving them in olive oil and garlic.

Madame Faravel pursed her lips and nodded assent. "I put up everything, the fruits, the vegetables, all we have to buy is sugar, coffee, meat, the staples . . . and, of course, our wine is from our own vineyards."

The idea of having his own wine was a clear call to arms for Paul-Marc, and he encouraged Monsieur Faravel to elaborate on his condition as a self-sustaining farmer. "We grow peaches, apricots, and what strawberries, green beans, tomatoes, and melons!"

Monsieur Faravel blew kisses of bliss to his garden, before falling back into the French rationale of the basic situation. "Ah, it is just as well, dear friends, when you think that we are forced to live on the miserable pension of a retired police officer. And my poor back, how it aches sometimes. I was wounded in the back, Monsieur Fabre. Your respected father, the Senator, got me my job, but after the accident we came back here to my family house."

"How I miss my Paris," sighed Madame Faravel, who obviously fancied the Champs-Élysées over the Grand' Rue of Vaison-la-Romaine.

"La Provence, elle est belle," shouted Monsieur Faravel,

full of winy sociability as he waved his arms in space, more or less in the direction of his holdings. With a high wall screening the valley, we could see nothing but the willow tree over our heads and the dark hills rising behind us. It occurred to me that a view is a modern device. Peasant houses turn their backs to a vale, to a range of hills folding into the sky, or to a seascape and its ever-changing mural of color and light. In Provence, the squat little houses deny the drift of vineyards spread like an embroidered cloak at their feet. Windows are square notches hacked through thick walls, their dense shutters opened only for the cool of the morning, then slammed against the blind sun, buckled against the "master wind," the famous mistral of Provence, that sweeps down from the north, stinging, embracing the valley in a grip of icy fingers. By definition, a house had to face south and turn its north shoulder to the gale. If the view happened to be southward, one was in luck.

The place I had seen further up the hill had that—a breathtaking view. But we were still in the formalities of paying a social call on the Faravels and I bit my tongue, holding back the urge to bring up the subject of the property that we had come to see.

The Faravels' house faced southeast with the structure L-shaped around the courtyard. No living-room or dining-room windows opened to the length of God's Plain, and the encasing walls were so high that we had to stand up to see over them.

"All that belonged to my father and now it belongs to me," said Monsieur Faravel pointing to the arc of vineyards, the cherry orchards, the vegetable garden as tidy as that of a *jardin de curé*. In the back rose a forest of pines cut by a creek and fed by springs which supplied his endless flow of precious water.

"Provence is unique," said Monsieur Faravel again, as though he had seen it for the first time.

"True," said Roger, "and our friends are thinking of buying a place here. The property next door, for instance, but I understand you guard it with your life."

Roger had finally raised the point of our visit, very subtly, as a matter of course. I wondered if Monsieur Faravel would react by showing a glimpse of his recognition of me as the stranger with the Balkan painter.

"I am the guardian," said Monsieur Faravel and put on his spectacles and gazed at me as though he just realized that I had been one of the trespassers of the day before.

"Ah, madame, you were here yesterday with that poacher. Forgive me, I didn't mean to frighten you but this is the third time he has broken into the place." Monsieur Faravel's voice mounted with anger.

"Méfiez-vous with that one," said Madame Faravel knifing the air with her hand. "The next time he will hear from the authorities."

"But he told me he owned the place," I protested.

"No, madame, he does not. The house belongs to people in Marseilles who never come here. I am the only person who has the key. If he prowls around here again, I will shoot off that gun in earnest. After all, in Paris I was a guard at the Quai d'Orsay." Faravel pounded his chest in pride.

"My friend is with the Quai," said Roger importantly.

"A member of the Ministry of Foreign Affairs? Well, that is different. But madame is not French, non?"

"I am American," I said rather timidly.

"It doesn't matter," Monsieur Faravel pronounced grandly. "Any member of the Foreign Office is a friend of mine. If you are interested in seeing the property, I'll get the keys." Faravel dashed into the house and came out with a pair of big iron keys on a chain.

"Is it like Chanteduc, our farmhouse above Vaison?" asked Régine.

"It is just a shambles," said Madame Faravel. "You stay here and tell me about your new place. The path up there is a jungle. You will tear your lovely silk dress. Did you get it in Paris?"

We left Régine and Madame Faravel talking about Chanteduc and Paris and dresses and followed Monsieur Faravel into the tangle of thickets that led to the pile of stones on the hill.

Monsieur Faravel had put on a straw hat for the climb and taken a scythe to slash away the underbrush. Paul-Marc, who had left his blazer and tie behind, rolled up his shirt sleeves and seemed ready to assault Kilimanjaro. Roger, the perfect *gentilhomme*, held the spiny branches aside for me as we trailed single file up the hill.

"The property begins at the edge of my vineyard. It used to be like our place when I was a boy, row after row of vines, and the richest olive grove in the region," said Faravel. "It is called Le Domaine des Michelons."

"So rich, with only one acre of land?" I asked.

"One acre, you say," said Faravel. "This entire hillside, north to that enormous tree, east to that farmhouse over there, west to my land, and south to that bouquet of pines. One acre . . . twelve acres is more like it. Did that rogue tell you one acre? You see, Monsieur Fabre, how people lie. He hoped to sell the house and parcel out the land to farmers. But he can't. I am the guardian here." Faravel rattled the keys.

We approached the round plateau of tall grass and the wall of cypress trees in front of the gray pavilion, ugly and jarring against the eighteenth-century stones. Faravel swept the cobwebs from the doorknob and turned a key in the latch. A shower of dust rained down as he heaved the door open to a concrete-floored room with raw plaster walls. Another square room led off to the south side, but there were no partitions for closets, or a bathroom, or a kitchen.

"The place was bought by people in Marseilles during the war to escape the bombs. Even then, the house was too ruined to live in so they had my brother-in-law build this pavilion. But he never finished it. The people only came once and then went back to the air raids. They missed the sea. Imagine that, Monsieur Fabre, for fifteen years now they've never visited their own house." Faravel shrugged in disbelief that anyone could possibly leave this place alone and unloved, a martyr to the scourge of wind and time. "The cypresses are dying too," he said, snapping off a fan of brittle leaves and crumbling it in his fingers. "But these walls are solid, they'll never tumble, a meter thick. They knew how to build in the old times." We all scraped our palms against the rough surface of the north wall as we clambered through the weeds around to the wooden portals under the lime tree. The sweetness of the yellow blossoms seemed to disinfect the fetid breath that yawned from the decayed cavity of the house.

Faravel flew into another rage when he saw the doors ajar. "What cheek, the cretin, an outrage . . ."

"Yes, he did force the lock," I said.

"You are a witness, madame, for the authorities," he said

ominously, and whipped his scythe through the blackberry bushes as though they were dandelions.

"Mon Dieu, it's the Dark Ages," said Paul-Marc, standing hands on hips and swiveling his eyes around the broken beams and buckled walls of the first room.

My heart sank. He is going to hate it, I thought. I should have described the worst instead of insisting on the beauty of the view. It was again the conflict of American and French attitudes. To me, the challenge of a ruin was grist to the mill of dreams, another chance to prove my unshakable faith in the future, the inborn persuasion of Americans that tomorrow's happiness will inevitably surpass that of today. Indulging a streak for reforming the world rather than accepting the human condition as it is, Paul-Marc would say, and dangerously lacking in French rationale.

Although I was still rather fuzzy as to exactly what the famous French rationale consisted of, I was certainly well attuned to my husband's lucidity and wit, a brilliance fortunately tempered by warmth and compassion for all living creatures. I often felt like a retarded kangaroo leaping to keep up with his wizardous mind. A product of the total sum of French education, he had degrees from the faculties of law and political science, a doctorate in economics, and had graduated from France's loftiest intellectual institution, L'École Nationale d'Administration. In the battle of Gallic and Anglo-Saxon cultures he had the jump on me too, having spent several years in London after fighting with the Free French air forces during the war. More fluent than flawless, my French was the result of two childhood years in a Monte Carlo convent that left me with a deceptively good accent but a wanting vocabulary. Whereas I could defend myself with effort in the crossfire of French conversation, Paul-Marc had English in perfect command. In American or British situations he thought in English. In French situations, in French. This was clearly a French situation, one which I had overblown with American verve. He admired my pioneering spirit, as he called it, but reason must dominate absurdity.

"This is not a *mas*, it's a mess," he pronounced. "Surely there must be places in better condition than this to buy around here."

"All these old farms need fixing up. You should have seen Chanteduc when we first found it," said Roger.

"It could be as beautiful as our house, monsieur. My nephew is a mason who lives down the road. In six months it could be like it used to be," said Monsieur Faravel. "I remember this place as a child. The old man, *le vieux*, who lived here loved me. He had the best olive groves in the Commune, and the best wine. And the most money. He never spent it. No. Thousands of gold francs he kept in a brown leather bag sewn into his bolster. He wanted to leave everything to me. The money, the goats, the mule. I can see that old mule now, hitched up back there in the stable. I used to come up every evening after school and help him feed grass to the rabbits and water the goats. Then we would sit by the oil lamp and talk. Right here, in the kitchen, next to the fire where it was warm. He was lonely. He wanted to live with us but my parents said no. When he fell ill, the public assistance came and got him and took all the money for his keep. He died there, *le pauvre vieux*. It was a shame, madame, to let him die like that. And I would have been rich. Imagine thousands of gold francs. Ah, it was a catastrophe, but, c'est la vie."

Paul-Marc and Roger investigated the hayloft upstairs and poked around in the stable and the cistern and decided that everything had to be renewed, except perhaps the exterior walls. Monsieur Faravel herded us up the east staircase to see a small low-ceilinged room where the old farmer used to sleep. Strangely, it was intact, with Provençal red-tiled floors and a gnarled olivewood banister. On the white plaster walls were odd markings of six vertical lines strophed diagonally through the middle. "The maquisards," said my husband, "that's how they kept a calendar of the days of the week."

"What an enchanting library this could be," I said.

"Not so much American zeal," said Paul-Marc; "let's see the rest."

The little house in the courtyard had two floors, with the rabbit hutches on the first, and dovecotes on the second. Remembering the bats, I merely glanced in from the corner of the door jamb, but could see that the rooms were perfectly square and well proportioned, and the rabbit hutch had in one corner a tall round stone oatbin.

"What about water?" asked Paul-Marc. "Does this place have the same rich source as yours?"

"Ah, water," said Faravel, "it is always a problem in Provence. There is no spring here, but a fine well. Of course the *vieux* could bathe in a glass of water. He used to pull it up in a bucket for the animals and drink a little himself. Here we drink mostly wine, monsieur."

We wandered down a path to the stony beehive of a well under another lime tree and peered into its depths. Paul-Marc tossed in a pebble and we heard the plunk quickly, which meant that it was almost full.

"God knows what's in there now. Probably a drowned

hare or two," laughed Monsieur Faravel. "We'll have to call
a well digger to clean it out and have the water analyzed in
Avignon."

"It rarely rains in summer. Water is a thing to watch when
buying here. We have two wells at Chanteduc," Roger said
proudly.

"In America we use masses of water, for washing that is,"
I added, already envisioning streams of friends pouring up
the road to visit.

"But here we do not, madame, this pure air, this clean
sky; we do not need it in Provence," said Monsieur Faravel.
"In any case, it's bad for the health, like night air."

"And electricity?" said Paul-Marc.

"Ah, yes, that you will have easily. We will go to see the
Mayor. The Commune will put it in for you. And a road,
too. I am sure of that," said Monsieur Faravel, who seemed
to take for granted that we would be his neighbors.

"No water, no road, no electricity, no ceilings, no floors,
no windows. Everything has to be done. It will take time
and money—lots of money," said Paul-Marc.

"But we can have it for a crumb, five thousand dollars
cash," I reminded him.

"That bloody liar," exclaimed Monsieur Faravel. "Is that
what he told you? Madame, only the land is worth a sou, the
house is a wreck. Trust me. We will go to Marseilles together
and see the owners. If they decide to sell, you'll have it for a
much better price."

The next morning Monsieur Faravel was to meet us in
Vaison on the Place du 11 Novembre, where the creamy
Postal, Telephone, and Telegraphic building backed up
against the sunken Quarter of the Villasse with its Roman
cobbles and sawed-off columns. We had walked through the

town to a café facing the shaded square. While Paul-Marc read the newspapers, I watched for Monsieur Faravel, who finally sped by, waved, and swerved his blue 2 CV between two tree trunks, carving a wide arc in the pink dust.

"Hello, I found the number in Marseilles," he said waving a sheet of paper as he crossed the street to join us.

"Bonjour," we said and all shook hands before Monsieur Faravel sat down and asked for a *pastis*. "Our drink of the Midi," he said as the waiter put a jigger of colorless liquid into a tall glass, then poured in water, giving it the look of green milk. Monsieur Faravel suggested we place the call at once as the lines were surely jammed and the post office closed down for two hours at noon for lunch.

We finished our drinks and sauntered over to the Poste, Télégraphe, Téléphone. Inside, a mad scramble of callers thrust and parried questions at a prim little woman who manipulated an archaic switchboard, yanking at the tangled trunklines as though they were coiled cobras. Her shrill voice sang above the din, "Your call to Aix, monsieur, in that booth on the right . . . Madame, if you please, be patient, Lyons is coming through . . . ne quittez pas, ne quittez pas . . . Mademoiselle, you have cut us off again . . . It will be an hour for Avignon . . ."

"Marseilles, if you please, Mademoiselle Lefêvre," said Monsieur Faravel, tipping his straw hat and handing her the number on a piece of paper.

"Bonjour, Monsieur Faravel," said Mademoiselle Lefêvre, pleased to see a familiar face. "I will place your call at once. Come back in half an hour."

The waiter swabbed the table and pulled out the wicker chairs as we returned to the Café of the Roman Ruins.

"The rotten telephone system accounts for half our customers. You'll have a good wait," he said taking our orders.

"Here we are in a cul-de-sac, at the end of the world," Monsieur Faravel explained. "A few tourists come, not too many because there is no train, only a bus a few times a day from Avignon. During the summer the hotel in Old Vaison fills up with people who know about our belles promenades, beaux sites, et bon repos. We have more sun here than in any other part of France. Ah, we have peace, madame, but, alas, our telephones!"

With the delicious ease of having nothing to do but wait we stretched our legs into the warm sun and watched the Vaisonais go by until we saw Mademoiselle Lefêvre waving from the steps of the PTT. With the spring of greased gazelles Paul-Marc and Monsieur Faravel leapt across the street and into the yellow house. Five minutes later they were back with the news that the son of Madame Leschi, the owner of the property, would see us that afternoon.

"Remember, we have made no firm decision yet," Paul-Marc warned me. "We must first be sure that the owner wants to sell and if so under what conditions."

I promised to let the Frenchmen do all the talking and we decided to leave right away, stopping briefly at the Fabre house to collect our convertible. An hour and a half of zig-zagging roads with Monsieur Faravel at the wheel of his bolting little Citroën, gesticulating, addressing his words to the back seat, seemed far too chancy an undertaking.

POSSESSION OF
A PILE OF STONES

. . . there is a little landscape
with a hovel, white, red, and green,
with a cypress beside it . . .

[VAN GOGH]

The wind combed our hair as we streaked down the road
that cuts through the heart of the Comtat Venaissin. Like il-
luminations from a Book of Hours, villages lay in golden
sleep on the swelling foothills of the Dentelles de Montmirail. Monsieur Faravel called this fretty range the Laces of
Gigondas, nicknamed for a hamlet cupped among its slopes
and the mettlesome little wine shed from its vineyards.

We drove on through the canal-laced town of L'Isle-sur-
la-Sorgue to the industrial center of Cavaillon. The scent of

melons mingled with the exhaust fumes of trucks carting straw-strewn cantaloupes to trains that would take them to the markets of Manchester and Mainz. At Salon, a dappling of plane trees locked horns across the main street shading us from the glare as we inched along behind a stream of cars. Michel de Nostradamus, who had lived there in the sixteenth century, now peered down in bronze magnificence from a plinth under a parasol of trees.

We passed the salty Lagoon of Berre with great shiny oil drums pitched like circus tents on its shore. A murmuration of jets spun around the runways of Marignane and the road sign read sixteen kilometers to Marseilles.

Faravel consulted his stainless-steel watch. "You are exactly one hour and a half from the Domaine des Michelons in Séguret to Marignane, that is to say two hours and a half from Paris. All the big jets stop here from Paris on their way to Africa. Monsieur, the plane is at your doorstep."

Soft puffs of briny air cut the heat. As we breached a hill the Mediterranean reached to the horizon, a flat blue carpet spread with a million mirror chips reflected in the sun. In the distance, Marseilles lay horizontal, hazy, and somnambulant.

We skirted the massive piers of the Grande Joliette. Tankers, liners, and cargo ships from all parts of the world were berthed in the great concrete wharves and a few hulking gray warships stood offshore.

In happy contrast the Vieux-Port looked like a Dufy water color. Fishing smacks, brightly painted and named for girls or saints, lay hull to hull against the cobbled quai and yachts waltzed at anchor on the blue floor. It was lunchtime and dizzying drifts of fish broth hung in the air. All around the Old

Port, awninged cafés and restaurants touted the business of bouillabaisse. We were famished and ready to stop at the first bistro, but Monsieur Faravel urged us on to his special place, where he knew the patron who would offer us the best fish stew and the coolest white wine in all Marseilles.

The patron met us like a character out of a Pagnol movie. Plump, with a fine Garibaldi mustache, he pumped our hands and led us out of the blare and the glare into the dark depths of his restaurant. We installed ourselves at a red-checked clothed table and perused the purple-inked menu. Bread and a carafe of wine were already there and the patron brought us a dish of pink shrimps to nibble. The napkins were white, large, and slightly damp.

"The menu is there," said the patron pointing with a flourish to a lighted tank where a variety of fish swam and dove. Beside it a small army of crustaceans squirmed on a bed of ice. "Une bouillabaisse, naturellement, messieurs, madame." In Marseilles, naturally.

Feeling wonderfully revived after lunch, we drove up La Canebière, the jumpy main street that stems off the Old Port. From the wide avenue we dipped into the tortuous narrow back streets, and eventually, after asking two traffic policemen, found the address of Monsieur Leschi. It was a graceful gray stone town house with tall windows and polished double doors on which a brass plaque read: *Maison de Redressement pour Jeunes Filles.*

"Is it a finishing school for young girls?" I asked, assuming Monsieur Leschi to be the headmaster.

Paul-Marc laughed out loud. "It is a school for wayward girls, poor little fallen angels who probably finished in the street."

We banged the brass knocker and an old woman in gray felt slippers let us into a dark tiled hallway. She opened the curtained glass doors to a shuttered sitting room and asked us to wait a few moments for Monsieur Leschi, who was expecting us. It was mercifully cool and so dark that we had to blink a minute before we could distinguish the big blue-plush chairs and sofa. I sank into one armchair, took off my dark glasses, and lit a Gauloise. Monsieur Faravel settled into the crook of the sofa and, silent for once, dozed off, doubtlessly feeling the need for his usual after-lunch siesta. Restless and active as always, Paul-Marc strode about the room like a black lion, peering at the contents of the bookshelves and cabinets. "This must be the first director of this admirable institution," he remarked, inspecting an enormous photograph in a gilt frame of a fiercely bearded gentleman. He plinked the keys of an old yellow-fanged upright piano respectably adorned with pronged appliqués and whistled a few bars of the "Marseillaise." That woke up Monsieur Faravel just in time, as the doors opened and in came Monsieur Leschi.

Unexpectedly handsome, he was tall, with crisp blue-gray hair, and sapphire-blue eyes, and he wore a blue suit. His handshake was firm. He seemed quite the contrary to his predecessor frowning down on us from the wall, and we felt immediately that the delinquent demoiselles were in good hands.

Monsieur Faravel leapt up and, as our agent and intermediary, took up the conversation, talking, as he always did, right into the face of Monsieur Leschi. He hoped Monsieur Leschi's mother, Madame Leschi, was well. He had spoken to her by telephone of our interest in their property in Séguret. And what luck for them to have him as their guardian, otherwise a Balkan knave would have sold it right out from under them. Monsieur Leschi said he was aware of this man and had never had the slightest intention of dealing with him. Naturally he would do nothing without consulting their good friend and neighbor Monsieur Faravel.

We nodded approval and Monsieur Faravel proceded to extoll our virtues as future owners of Le Domaine des Michelons. We were prepared to restore the property. Monsieur Leschi and Madame Mère would cry if they could see the sorry state into which it had fallen. The house a ruin, tumbling to the ground. The land snarled with fallen trees and overgrown brush. The olive groves blighted by the 1956 freeze and the vineyards gone to seed. No one would pay a centime for the house itself, only the land had value, and very little at that. It would take years of cultivation before it yielded a bean, much less a grape or a goblet of wine. Why, Monsieur Faravel wanted to know, had the Leschis let their property run down, why had they never come back to the beautiful Vaucluse?

It was a family problem, Monsieur Leschi told us. A strange destiny had befallen them. One that made it impossible for any one of the Leschis to travel that far by car, and that was the only way to get there. Every time they took a motor trip, they had an accident. Not just a simple one, but a fatal crash. Ten members of the family had been killed on the road. Five cars had been smashed to pieces. Now his mother refused to go anywhere in a car. Her husband had perished at the wheel of his Renault. She had inherited the house in the Vaucluse when he died. It was very sad for they had bought it together and she had named the place for her husband, Sérafin. We would see on the deed that to the name of the property, "Le Domaine des Michelons," had been added "La Sérafine." He was from Corsica and that was the reason for the spelling.

Perhaps, Monsieur Faravel thought, he should come and see it before deciding definitely to part with the place, although, of course, he repeated, Monsieur Leschi would be shocked, scandalized, outraged at the catastrophe.

Monsieur Leschi apparently did not need such a hard sell, as he stated that under the circumstances he and his mother had decided to dispose of the property. He realized that only the land could be considered valuable and felt that a fair asking price would be one million five hundred thousand old francs.

The papers, he said, were with a Marseilles notary, whom he would call so that we could stop by his office to start the arrangements for the settlement. We thought that sounded agreeable. Paul-Marc wrote a note of our good faith. He was so incredibly surprised to find Monsieur Leschi's price so much less than we expected, three thousand dollars instead of the Balkan's five, that he jumped at it. Pure impulse buying. We had no idea about the taxes, the costs of restoration, the permissions to replant the vineyards, the legal entanglements. In fifteen minutes we had become the owners of a property in Provence. Or so we thought.

The Marseilles' notary's office was a far cry from that of his colleague in Vaison-la-Romaine. Pretty girls, their long hair streaming, their skirts pulled tight over their mandolin-round bottoms, skated across the parquet, too busy with papers and errands to notice us. Eventually Paul-Marc made it clear that we had an appointment. His card produced prompt action and the notary received us in his modern black-and-white office. A secretary was dispatched to find the file on La Sérafine while he noted the details of the transaction. Naturally there would be legal moves. It was a complicated procedure. The notary in Sablet had the original bill of sale, which would have to be traced. He would let us know when to return to Marseilles to sign the papers, probably in August.

Obviously, the sale of this obscure cheap farmhouse was very small potatoes to the notary, a dapper, sleek-haired man no doubt used to negotiating far more expensive sun-traps on the Côte d'Azur. Furthermore, the fact that we had decided for personal reasons to have the property in my name shocked him profoundly. Napoleon's rigidly misogynous Civil Code of 1804 was still firmly in sway, which to my amazement as an American meant that a woman could not own property without the permission of her husband. In fact, any property or inheritance a wife brought to the marriage became joint ownership, administered by the husband. Any earnings became communal, and a woman was permitted a passport, a bank account, or a job *only* with the consent and signature of her lord and master. To see a sturdy Frenchman turning over his legal domination to a woman, especially an American one, unnerved the meridional notary. When La Sérafine's dusty file was finally unearthed, he leafed through the weathered documents. We produced passports, letters of credit, and bank references, and the notary witnessed the heinous act as my husband signed a statement for the property to be put in my name.

BONDS OF
FRIENDSHIP

*. . . Soul that speaks through the rushing
waters of the Rhône and its winds.
Soul of the echoing woods,
the sun-drenched shores . . .*

[MISTRAL, *Calendal*]

After our return to Paris we spent the month of July planning our August holidays in Provence. With their usual hospitality, Roger and Régine Fabre had offered us the use of
Chanteduc and Paul-Marc invited his father to join us.
By Régine's exacting standards, her farmhouse was still too
primitive to be lived in but we were delighted to rough it at
Chanteduc. Five miles north of Séguret, it was an excellent
base of operations for shaping plans for our new property.
In Paris I had been clipping pictures of kitchens and bath-

rooms and collecting books on Provençal design. With un-quelled American exuberance and excessive confidence in the Midi temper, I dreamed of spending Christmas in the cozy warmth of our Provençal farmhouse.

Of course Paul-Marc pointed out with relentless French realism that we had not yet signed the deed to the property. Nevertheless, our commitment was firm and as the Faravels' entrepreneur nephew was prepared to draw up estimates, we thought we might as well get started. One more winter of furious mistral winds snapping down from the Alps through the Rhône Valley might demolish La Sérafine altogether.

We made the nine-hour drive from Paris to Provence at a stretch, stopping only for lunch in the Beaujolais country. In Avignon we picked up my father-in-law, who had come by train from Bayonne to meet us. He felt a change from the iron-damp air of the Atlantic coast to the dry sun of Provence would be healthful, and we found him waiting in the Buffet de la Gare sipping an apéritif and reading a newspaper. His black violin case lay on the table. Beau-Père never budged without his violin which, depending upon the state of his mind and his liver, he played passably to perfectly well. For him, a day without music was a day without food, both of which he held in equal esteem. Although he looked small and fragile enough to be swept away by a whiff of the mis-tral, he was a whirlwind of energy and shared with his son an absorbing interest in politics and an endless capacity for conversation. Undaunted by the long train ride across France, he said it was like the métro as he kissed each of us on both cheeks.

We packed him and his violin into the car and skimmed out of Avignon, past the crenelated walls and into the mainstream of August motorists heading from Paris to the French Riviera. At the village of Courthezon we cut out of the din and into the peaceful shade of the plane-roofed square where we stopped for provisions. Each one went in a different direction, to the creamery, the butcher, the winery, the bakery, until we had enough food for a proper French meal. A mauvy haze of twilight settled over God's Plain as we drove through one quiet village after another to the road that skirts the Ouvèze River flowing through Vaison-la-Romaine. At the Roman bridge we curled up the hill by the fortress until we breached another hill and the rocky road leading to Chanteduc. Overhanging branches scratched the paint and swallowed up the car in shadows as we tunneled past a deserted farmhouse and onto the plateau where Chanteduc sat like a ginger fortress on a table of grass.

Named for the great predator owl, Chanteduc looked more an aerie for hoot owls. It had all the endearments of miniature things. A high wall embraced its square rooms built of roughhewn stone. To the north, umbrella pines framed the high windswept peak of Mont Ventoux, its bald pate wreathed in a laurel of cloud. All around, a green lake of vineyards lapped at the jut of rock where Chanteduc perched, prey to sun, wind, and sky, and like its namesake, swiveled its head full circle to a view of four *départements* of France.

We unloaded the luggage and Paul-Marc swung open the wooden portals to a courtyard feathered in weeds. The peasants who built Chanteduc must have been very small. The beams almost brushed our hair in the living room with its white plaster chimneypiece and its north window crisscrossed with iron bars. Arched like an entrance to a cave, the stone stairwell curved up to the bedrooms. An enormous polished armoire took up most of the upper hall and up three more steps we found our room, the largest in the house, with a wide chintz-covered bed, a red straw rug, and a chest of drawers.

Beau-Père's room faced south, a sliver of a room with just enough space for a single bed, a table, and a chair. More steps led to a turret and a hayloft, which like the rest of the house was paved in meridional tomato-red tiles and beamed with solid rafters. With her genius for organization, Régine Fabre had urged the busy plumber in Vaison to transport a complete bathroom up the hill and install it in a square pink room. I had a spray shower while Paul-Marc and Beau-Père went out to look around the property as the last rays of sun slid behind the mountains.

Except for the monotonous swing of the pendulum and the metronome tick of the grandfather's clock in the living room, a pall of stillness shrouded the house. A hairy brown centipede slipped behind the refrigerator as I switched it on and unpacked our cartons of food. Everything was loose or stuck in a cone of newspaper. One of the eggs had broken in its wrapping of *Le Figaro*, sliming up the rest, and the white asparagus had left a dusting of sand on the peaches. I laid the dining table with orange mats and napkins, tilting the cutlery on knife holders, placing a wineglass near each pottery plate. After washing the salad, I stuffed it into a metal basket and swung it dry in the courtyard.

Night had fallen like a lid on a pot. Where are the men? I wondered, suddenly more nervous than serene at being left alone on this faraway hilltop. Once the sun went down it all looked so bleak. I began to panic at the thought of weeks on end in a lonely country house. Wouldn't the time drag for people like us used to the excitement of cities or resorts? At the Fabres' town house, there was always the nearness of cafés and the lights of Vaison, but up here the darkness was complete, the silence deafening. Everything seems strange at first, I convinced myself, and set about making the living room more inviting by lighting candles and putting a tray of whisky and Perrier water on a table in front of the fireplace. I switched on the transistor. Lights. Music. That was more like it. Instantly the stony hovel for midget peasants became a cozy pleasance for Parisians dining on top of the world.

The men whistled as they came through the courtyard. I rushed to greet them. "Formidable," said Paul-Marc embracing me. "You've made the place enchanting."

"At last you're here. Do have a drink, you must have walked for miles."

"We've been all around the place," said Paul-Marc stamping the dust from his heels. "The well is full, the vines are flourishing, and the woods are alive with nightingales."

"You can see every star in the sky," said Beau-Père. "But the air is almost too dry. I am used to the Atlantic breeze and a town full of lights and cafés. Yes, it is beautiful, mes chers enfants, but we are at the end of the world."

He was echoing my thoughts of a few minutes before, but Paul-Marc would have none of it. "À table, à table, nous ne sommes pas ici pour rigoler!" he urged, as food in France is no laughing matter.

After the main course and the better part of a chilled bottle of white Châteauneuf-du-Pape, Beau-Père was liking Provence a bit better, but still he hoped that the property we had bought was in better shape than this one, that it was not so remote, and it would not cost us an arm and a leg to restore. We dared not tell him that Chanteduc was a palace compared to La Sérafine. He would see for himself soon enough.

Bonds of Friendship

Dawn breaks early in summertime Provence. Beau-Père was up with it and had his bowl of *café au lait* before beginning his morning concert of Lalo's Spanish Symphony. The silver screech of strings awakened us and we went downstairs to find him standing before his score. "The acoustics are excellent," he exclaimed playing a few more bars.

"Bravo, Beau-Père, you look like Toscanini and you play like Paganini. Did you sleep well?"

"Not very well. The air is as dry as a bone and the bed is as hard as a rock. We had such a light dinner last night, I'm afraid I ate all the croissants!" Beau-Père laughed, very proud of his healthy appetite.

"It is Sunday and the market is open only in the morning," he reminded us, suggesting some of the Provençal delicacies to stock up on, and of course, mineral water. He certainly did not trust the cool spring water that flowed from the well.

"We are more interested in seeing Monsieur Faravel," said Paul-Marc. "He is waiting with his nephew, the entrepreneur, who has given up his Sunday sleep to look over the house with us."

We put the top of the car down and keeled off into the sun, lunging down Chanteduc's shoals to the vibrant streets of Vaison-la-Romaine. The Merovingian church tolled its booming call to the faithful as we swung onto the valley road leading to the dusty climb to the Faravels. Monsieur Faravel was waiting at the gate of his house in his rakish straw hat and his dark Sunday suit. He did not go to Mass, but on Sunday he wore his best.

"Bonjour, bonjour," he greeted us warmly, asking us to stay on for lunch after inspecting the property.

Beau-Père accepted at once. In the back of his mind was

the dire realization that we had bought no food in Vaison. Everything would be shut tight until Monday and we had passed no promising restaurants on the road. Paul-Marc banked the car against the curve and secured the wheels with boulders. Beau-Père found a knobby branch to use as an alpine stick and we began the plod up to La Sérafine. By now we had become quite accustomed to the rigors of the clamber, but Beau-Père exclaimed constantly . . . no road, not even a foot path. Could this exist in civilized Provence?

Monsieur Faravel went ahead and waved us into the open round in front of the house. The scraggly crescent of cypress trees still stood but the high grass had been razed flat. When we went around to the courtyard the doors opened easily because the brambles had been scythed and cleared. Bless Faravel. He had cleaned the spiky softening wreath of greenery leaving us access to the house, but in the process he had unmasked the monster. If La Sérafine had seemed a draped novice about to be beatified, she now appeared a martyr on the faggots, shaved, denuded, a heap of gray bones. A few fallen shutters hung twisted from their hinges, blistered walls showed patches of rot, the terrace was a mass of ant-eaten beams.

"She is clean," said Faravel proudly.

"What a catastrophe. It is unlivable!" Beau-Père raged at the sight. "Squandering the family patrimony. This sort of thing happened before when your cousin Philippe bought a ruin in Auvergne. He thought he could grow orchards from cherry pits. What a fool! It's true that Grandfather on my mother's side retired at the age of thirty-five. But he had great holdings in Normandy. What apple trees, what Calvados! But this place has nothing . . . rien . . . rien . . . rien."

"My dear Beau-Père, come and look at the little rooms. How sweet they will be when they are plastered and beamed and tiled. You can have a concert hall all to yourself," I said taking him inside.

"But my pauvre petite," he droned. "You are an American. Americans are said to be sensible people. Surely you must see the folly of all this. Une pure folie."

"Come look at the view. That's God's Plain down there. About the house, one must have a bit of imagination."

"Imagination, my dear, yes, and many, many francs. And many, many dollars. You Americans are young and enthusiastic. In France we have seen so much, war, occupation, inflation. In the last war our house in the Loire Valley was bombed to the ground. In the first war the family lost a fortune in Russian bonds. In the Franco-Prussian War the people of Paris were so starved they ate rats. One of my ancestors spent twenty years in Austria after the Napoleonic campaigns!" Beau-Père took the cagey French point of view of life that nothing could be so bad that it couldn't be worse. My unbridled American optimism for the bigger, better, happier tomorrow wearied him.

"You have no philosophy," he said. "In France we are taught a basic Cartesian truth and made to prove it rationally. In my opinion this is une grande folie. Remember Descartes. I think therefore I am. Je pense donc je suis . . . je pense donc je suis!"

Monsieur Faravel stood mesmerized by the erudition and eloquence of Beau-Père, who waved his alpine stick at the house as though by magic it would vanish like the crashing chords at the end of a symphony. But instead of the house disappearing, Robert Charrasse appeared. He swaggered into the courtyard, a handsome bulky young man, his black eyes shining like ripe olives. None of the dark Sunday best for Robert. He wore narrow beige slacks, a navy-blue jersey, and a gold watch on his hairy wrist.

"You see, I have come on Sunday." He pronounced *dimanche* in the slurred Provençal way, *demayncha.*

We all shook hands. Robert Charrasse was sympathetic from the start. Young, modern, and dynamic, he was the new Provençal, a man who believed in getting things done. Paul-Marc took to him instantly and they went straight to the business at hand. We trailed behind them through the dank rooms as Robert thumped the walls and sounded the ceilings. He measured door openings, gazed up the chimney flue and waded through the dust of the cave. On the terrace he stamped his feet up and down to test the solidity of the foundations. "This used to be part of the stable. Part of the roof collapsed leaving what appears to be a terrace. It is not solid."

The little house in the courtyard he diagnosed as equally ailing, but thought we could count on the outside walls of both buildings. Except for that everything would have to be restored from the ground up. Why then, he wanted to know, didn't we tear it all down and build a new bungalow like his. It was modern, with square rooms, steel shutters, bright tiles, and a big bathroom. It would cost no more to have a completely new place than to put this wreck back together again.

I had noticed the Charrasse house at the entrance to the road. A depressingly uniform structure with no view and a massive garage.

"Monsieur Charrasse," I said, "we like this place because it is a ruin, an eighteenth-century pile of stones. We want to restore it as it is. I can see it all. Three bedrooms and two bathrooms up there, a library in that little room, a kitchen . . ."

"Not so fast," cautioned Paul-Marc. "We will start with the essentials, roof, walls, stones, and mortar. Then you may plan the rooms as you like."

"I want it to be in character. As Provençal as bouillabaisse."

"Madame," said Robert Charrasse, "I am the one who rebuilt the village of Séguret. It is a poem of Provençal planning. For generations we have been builders and I am a stonemason like my father before me."

"Bien sûr," Paul-Marc assured Robert and asked him to draw up a plan and give us an approximate idea of what the restoration would involve.

"Don't sign anything until you sleep on it. A catastrophe, a catastrophe," muttered Beau-Père in a kind of recitative as he strode down the hill.

"It is good that you will restore this property. It has been a blight on the landscape," said Robert. "I had no idea it had fallen into such a state of dilapidation. It has been years since anyone has been near the place."

"I could have told you all about it, my dear nephew," said Monsieur Faravel. "But you never come to see us any more. How is the family? Your wife, the little boys, your mother, your father, your grandmother?"

"The family is well, thank you, Uncle," Robert replied hurriedly before leaping into his swift yellow DS Citroën and speeding down the hill.

"He's going up fast. Perhaps too fast, that young one. Someday he may have to swallow water snakes," said Monsieur Faravel, using the French equivalent for eating crow, probably because crow in dire moments can be eaten in casserole, whereas serpents have not yet been put to the boil. We trailed down the sun-baked lane to the Faravel house as Madame came out of the kitchen door drying her hands on her apron.

"Come in where it is cool. I'll bring the *pastis*. Are you still so taken with the domain in this summer heat?" asked Madame Faravel, her voice tinged with sarcasm.

"Chère madame, I think they have fallen on their heads," said Beau-Père pulling up a chair to the kitchen table while Madame Faravel reshined the glistening glasses and placed them on the plastic floral cloth. "Now if it were a charming house like yours," said Beau-Père gallantly, plainly pleased with Madame Faravel and to be within arm's reach of a fresh drink and the gratifying aromas wafting from the stove.

"Thank you, monsieur." Madame Faravel bestowed a dazzling smile on Beau-Père as she poured the *pastis*, lifting her elbow to reveal the furry depths of her armpit. She looked pale and cool in her yellow dress, a black-eyed Susan in her spotless white kitchen. She wagged a finger at me warningly. "You, madame, so fair and with no straw hat. You will have a sunstroke from this heat. For your husband it is all right. He is as dark as a Provençal but you are already burned as pink as a prawn and there are freckles on your nose!" She called them lentil spots and wrinkled her own flawless nose distastefully.

"Would you like to wash up?" asked Monsieur Faravel, anxious for me to see the upper floor and the modern bathroom. He led the way up the spiral staircase to a corridor cut by closed doors. He opened one to show me the guest room with a suite of shiny satinwood furniture before opening the door to the bathroom. "Monsieur Bonell installed it. He is a fine plumber and electrician. He will put one in for you just like this." The room was long with a tall window that looked over God's Plain. The tub seemed big enough to swim in and was white like the other fixtures. Monsieur Faravel seemed loath to depart. "Of course you will not have as much water as we do. As rare as a jewel, water, madame. I had this bathroom installed when I inherited the house. My father didn't believe in such extravagances. Mother used to boil the well water in a big kettle on the stove and we used to bathe in the kitchen in front of the wood stove where it was warm in winter. In summer I used to swim in the river or dive in the watering basin. But Madame Faravel is a Parisian. She likes everything to be perfect. So Monsieur Bonell put in his best bathroom for us and an electric heater so the water would be hot night and day. We have le tout confort, madame."

I used *le tout confort* with great pleasure, splashing cold water on my lentil spots and dipping my bitten feet into the bidet. When I came downstairs Beau-Père was hovering over the pretty frizzed head of Madame Faravel as she basted the lamb with a glass of red wine. "There is every reason to believe that Madame is a great chef," he said before offering the advice that we all get to the table at once. Paul-Marc, hardly less immune to the herbaceous sizzle, finished his drink and we filed into the dining room.

Next door to the kitchen, the dining room was shadowed and fresh. Cracked shutters let in slits of light that fell over the white linen table cloth, the starched napkins, and Madame Faravel's best china. The Faravels obviously did not believe in any of the peasant country touches. The room was the soul of bourgeoisie with a heavy buffet covered with a crocheted runner, high-backed golden-oak chairs cushioned in brown leather, and polychrome prints of Notre-Dame de Paris, the Arc de Triomphe, and La Place de la Concorde. In one corner stood a vase of bright, stiff-petaled zinnias from Madame Faravel's cutting garden. There were no flowers on the snow-clean cloth. That was reserved for the dishes of black olives, hard round sausage, vinegared cucumbers, and pâté of thrush. Monsieur Faravel poured *rosé* wine into the smaller of the two glasses at each place.

"To our new neighbors. To new heights of friendship in Franco-American relations!" he proclaimed raising his glass to our health. We drank solemnly. To *la France*. To *l'Amérique*. Monsieur Faravel leaned back on the legs of his chair relishing his role as master of the house and country squire. Madame Faravel whisked the empty dishes off the table and brought in hot dinner plates. Then she presented us with a view of the *gigot,* crusted brown and steamy, before taking it back to the kitchen to be carved in thick bloody slices. Monsieur took the bottles of red wine off the buffet where they had been left open to breathe. He poured a soupçon for himself and tasted it, curling his tongue over his lips in satisfaction before half filling our glasses. Madame Faravel brought in the platter of lamb and an earthenware casserole of white beans sprinkled with parsley and herbs.

"Excellent, superb, delicious," extolled Beau-Père as he cut the lamb with his fine musician's hands.

"For one so small and as thin as a nail, your father does not lack appetite," said Madame Faravel, delighted with the success of her cooking. "I can see that Monsieur has le bec fin. He is right, this lamb is the very best to be found in all of France."

Monsieur Faravel explained that in spring the Provençal

shepherds herded their flocks to the slopes of Mont Ventoux to graze on sprigs of wild fennel, thyme, and marjoram. The perfume was built in, heightened by a few cloves of garlic slipped in by Madame Faravel.

"From our garden," said Monsieur Faravel when Madame brought in the next course of salad greens. "Oil from our olives and vinegar from our wine." The small laurel-wrapped cakes of ewe's milk cheese he had to admit came from the village of St.-Marcellin. "Right, never the creamy Camembert or Brie in summer. Too ripe, too hard on the liver," said Beau-Père slicing into the pebbly curd. As usual in France, after the appetite has been sated with the main course, conversation sprints into high gear with the cheese, and Monsieur Faravel waxed warm in praise of his way of life.

It was not always easy. Often there were problems, too much spring rain for the grapes, too much summer heat for the fruit trees. Strikes were a perpetual hazard, especially when the railroad stopped and tons of produce rotted on the platform before ever reaching the markets of Les Halles in Paris. Middlemen reaped most of the profits in any case. The ministers in Paris did little to protect the poor farmer who did all the work and took all the risks. Still there were compensations. No luxuries, but they had a small car, a radio, and a fine house which we could see, with running water and electricity and a Mazout stove in the kitchen against the winter cold. Occasionally there was a shopping trip to Avignon, and once every two years a fortnight in Paris with Madame Faravel's mother. Madame Faravel's sister came with her husband and children from Lille to visit in the summer and her mother came in the autumn. Still Madame Faravel missed Paris. She felt an outsider in Séguret. The family had not been exactly welcoming as there had been a good deal of jealousy about his getting the house and land at his father's death. But Monsieur Faravel loved Provence, his home was Séguret, and all things considered, Madame Faravel had adapted well. She was a perfect country wife. She had learned to feed the chickens leftover bread and to collect grass for the rabbits. She did the laundry in the big cold-water granite tub in the garage, cooked all the delicious Provençal dishes, cleaned the house, and had her dog and cat for company. They had an electric refrigerator, and the wine kept fresh in the cold cellar. There was always a chicken or a guinea fowl or a duck that he would ax and Madame would deplume and roast. In the fall, they took their baskets and went hunting the reddish-brown mushrooms that sprouted wild around the tree trunks of our domain. If things got tight, there would always be eggs laid by their hens for an omelette with truffles sniffed out by their wiry little dog. And then there was the beauty of Provence, the sun, the clean air. No, all in all it was not a bad life, Monsieur Faravel decided philosophically. Madame Faravel agreed it was not a bad life, but it would be better now that they had neighbors from Paris just up the hill.

The afternoon was deepening into evening when we left the Faravels. They pressed a bottle of wine on us and we invited them for lunch at Chanteduc. As we drove back through the valley, I no longer wondered how we would pass the time in the country. There were stirrings of life in the stones of La Sérafine; bonds of friendship had been sealed. But most astonishing of all was the charm and generosity of the Faravels, who could offer us such abundant hospitality on a retired police officer's income of one hundred and twenty dollars a month.

VI

BUILDING THE ARK

*It will have white walls
with a decoration of great yellow
sunflowers. . . . In the morning
when you open the window
you will see the green of gardens
and the rising sun . . .*

[VAN GOGH]

For the next two weeks we shuttled from the peaks of Chanteduc to the ruins of La Sérafine, starting out in the early morning before the sun rained down its shower of singeing rays. Monsieur Faravel usually bounded out of his house as we passed to join us and offer his voluble opinions on the rebuilding of the house. One of the rare totally unskeptical Frenchmen, Monsieur Faravel was the exact opposite of Beau-Père, whom we often left to chat with Madame Faravel. Whereas Monsieur Faravel bubbled with joy at the rapid, precise decisions of Paul-Marc, Beau-Père was eating out his liver and ours. He piped a continual tune of despair and when we stopped listening he would perch on a fallen beam, throw back his head and address his muttered indignation to the sky. Beau-Père preferred the company of Madame Faravel, who listened, and even better, agreed, for the most part, that we had bitten off more than we could chew. Madame Faravel in no way resented us as intruders, but felt that the people of Séguret would be as reluctant to accept us as they had been to accept her. She looked upon us as allies from Paris, natural champions of her cause in her personal feud with her Séguret in-laws. She hinted darkly to Beau-Père that it would not surprise her to find us the targets of a good fleecing by Robert Charrasse. Fortunately he was her husband's nephew and they were close enough to keep an eye on him. After all, had it not been for the Faravels we would have been taken in by that unscrupulous Balkan. The painter had left the region and the local notary had not seen fit to mention the matter of the property having been negotiated through the offices of another notary. Although Madame Faravel kept her counsel with her neighbors, she knew everything that went on.

We had no such misgivings about Robert Charrasse. We liked him and he plainly approved of us. Prosperity was in the air. We had decided, and Paul-Marc had made it clear, that we wanted all the work on the house done by the artisans of Séguret. Every franc for the reconstruction of our house was to be fed into the local economy.

"In-put, out-put," Paul-Marc had explained while we discussed the renovation of the house one night at Chanteduc. "If the villagers benefit from our investment, the village will prosper, and in turn, we will become a part of their life and not just summer visitors. It is best to work with Charrasse and the local people." I had to agree with him. Of course, he was right and, as Beau-Père pointed out, I knew absolutely nothing of French systems. If we insisted on going through with this foolishness, at least let my husband handle it. *Les femmes* have no head for such matters, *les maris* must decide. I submitted to his advice, rather humbly, I thought, just offering a few suggestions about the final design.

"Please, let's try to keep as many of the original features as possible. I love the old beams and tiles. We don't want our farmhouse in the Vaucluse to look like a new villa on the Riviera, do we?" I was thinking of the house Robert Charrasse had built for his own family, and of the Faravels' place, which they had done their best to disguise as stuffy middle-class. "Provençal charm and American convenience." Beau-Père liked that and Paul-Marc promised to back me up if it came to an issue, although he felt my fears of Robert's being too *jeune, moderne et dynamique* ungrounded.

A few days before, Robert Charrasse had taken us to see his restoration of the village of Séguret, leading us through the narrow coiling lanes he had repaved. He had relaid the squat stone pillars holding the steep tiled roof of the communal laundry basin and indented a rim of stone benches into the wall surrounding the Square of the Shields. Over filaments of wire he had trained thick-leafed branches of plane trees, giving the square the look of a country ballroom decorated for a *fête champêtre*. But with no revelers. Except for a woman scrubbing and wringing her wash at the laundry fountain, the cobbled paths were as still as those on a postcard. No sound filtered through the shutters of ocher houses. There were no stores, no cafés, no children playing, no cats purring in the sun, no old men playing *boule*.

The tour of Séguret, however, had proven to us that Robert harbored a love and respect for Provençal architecture even though he identified himself with the emerging generation of technocrats. He had such humor and agility and winning charm that any clash of ideas would be fought in a spirit of gamesmanship. For all his cocksure confidence in himself, Robert was as supple as a Marseilles sailor.

No blueprint was needed to convince us of the floor plan for La Sérafine. The peasants who had lived there for centuries had added on lopsided wings and wedges of roofs as though, like their vines, they had been planted and grafted and grown. Those canny peasants, with the same infallible sense of a spider for its web, had spun for us a unique design. Their oatbins and dovecotes, mangers and goat stalls, caves and haylofts would convert for us into a house—a house like no other. To keep its character, our *mas* would have to zigzag and rise and fall with the hillside to which it clung, clamped there implacably for two hundred or more years.

"Eh bien," Robert said. "I will be your architect and your builder. First the roof. We'll have to repave it with beautiful bright orange tiles. Made like the old ones, but shiny and new." Paul-Marc and I looked at each other. We loved the weathered pink and gold clay that deflected mauve shadows or caught the sunlight and melted almost imperceptibly into the colors of the earth.

"Couldn't you reinforce the roof from underneath and use these tiles again?" Paul-Marc asked.

"Do you mean you really want these *old* things?"

Clearly the *jeune, moderne et dynamique* side of Robert Charrasse was outraged. Provençal patterns were one thing, but out-of-date Provençal materials were another. He strode about pounding the walls. The long gray windowless north wall looked solid and Robert felt that it would hold. Jagged blocks of stone showed through the south wall, *pierres apparentes,* the chunky rock surfaces marking the ancient vintage of these farmhouses.

"May we keep the walls like this, Robert?"

"As crumbly as a fresh croissant," he replied, flaking the mortar under his hairy fist. "How drôle that you an American, madame, should want your house to look *old!*"

The interior walls were uneven, curving slightly, cut here and there with odd, unexpected niches, perhaps for a madonna or an oil lamp. Obviously all of the cracked surfaces would have to be troweled and plastered and smoothed, but Robert promised me the old niches. The windows were another matter.

To us they seemed depressingly small with only a shaft of light allowed to enter from the south and none at all from the north. From all the southern windows the view dipped down the hillside to God's Plain.

"Open the windows. We want the light, the sun, the view!" Paul-Marc instructed.

"No, no," said Monsieur Faravel. "The sun will fade everything."

"You are not from the Midi, monsieur, you can not imagine the wildness of the north wind," said Robert.

"But we can not live in a dungeon. Stretch them by fifty centimeters." For once we did not want those old things.

Robert stepped off the main front room kicking up a spray of dust as he measured the floor.

"This will be a fine roomy kitchen, bright and sunny," suggested Monsieur Faravel. "You can take out this ancient granite sink and put in a white enamel one like ours. To think, I used to sit right here by the fire with the old farmer and now I will be visiting right here again with you!"

"You will, of course, Monsieur Faravel, but this large entrance hall will be the living room for now," I replied. "I'm afraid we'll have to put the kitchen back there in the cave."

"Back there? Impossible . . . madness. That is the north wall. You will freeze and, besides, there is no window and no place for a table to sit around when friends come to call."

"In America we have compact kitchens with all the equipment along one wall. Everything mechanical, very convenient. We'll just cut a window there and have a glass of wine here by the fireplace . . . in the salle de séjour."

Robert sided with his uncle against the moist cave and thought the kitchen should be in the south-facing square room once the cistern was removed. "Perfect for a dining room, too good for the kitchen," I insisted, and Paul-Marc let me decide, although both Robert Charrasse and Monsieur Faravel were scandalized by his submissiveness. A Frenchman should assert authority, especially in the matter of the superlative of French civilization: food. In Provence, the cuisine is the heart of the house; the *foyer*, the hearth.

Men should choose wives and cattle from their own country, I could see Monsieur Faravel thinking as we peered into the cobwebbed cave, which seemed remote even to me as the functional, all-along-one-wall kitchen I envisioned. I still thought of the kitchen as an American invention, a heaven of mechanical gadgets, and a place to get in and out of as quickly as possible.

The upstairs rooms were to be bedrooms, so there was little argument except about the disposition of space and exposure. Paul-Marc wanted the sloping hayloft ceiling restored and beamed, the casement window widened, and the sagging floor leveled and paved. The room of the maquisards, perfect in its square proportions, could be restored as easily as the room of the *vieux*, with its olivewood banister and wooden-latched window. The long north room where the winter vegetables had been stored we decided to slice into three parts as a bath, a hall, and a bedroom. Monsieur Faravel raised cries of protest as we designed the window openings, predicting frozen water pipes and a bedroom too glacial for winter habitation. Robert conceded, however, that it might be *moderne, jeune et dynamique* to break with Midi convention and, for once, defy the north wind.

"I will reset the staircases with smooth flagstones," said Robert as we slipped down the rounded steps to the future living room.

"No, please, leave these old stones," I said, but Robert, fixing me with his deep brown gaze, reminded me firmly that we would break our necks if we didn't have them changed.

Robert Charrasse had his crew of artisans lined up. Gilec Aymard, the carpenter, was from the region. He lived not in Séguret, but in Sablet, the village which had become almost Spanish with the influx of migrant workers.

Monsieur Aymard met us at the house one day, a brawny young man with wavy carrot-colored hair, freckles, and green eyes. He had a hard handshake, a soft sweet smile, and a deep voice that inspired confidence. Although a deep-rooted Provençal, he had, like Robert Charrasse, firm convictions of what was *jeune, moderne et dynamique.*

"These beams," Paul-Marc said, "would be attractive on the ceilings of the living room."

Gilec Aymard kicked them disdainfully and a colony of ants spewed from their ridges.

"You don't want those old things," he said. "They are full

of termites." Ironically, the restoration of La Sérafine was becoming a battle between us living in the New World wanting the old and the Provençaux of the Old World wanting the new.

An ancient olivewood shaft, dark and corded with a wide screw in its center, supported the low ceiling between the living room and the cave.

"The farmer brought in his olive press and made the oil here," Monsieur Faravel explained as we examined it. Rutted and uneven, but strong and seemingly eternal, the beam remained. After measuring the windows Monsieur Aymard agreed to enlarge and shutter them with iron-locked wooden panels. He would salvage the weatherbeaten front door and I asked to have it sliced in half, like a Normandy stable door, so that we could have more sunlight. All the bedroom doors would have to be carved and fitted with jambs and hardware. The tall creaky portals leading to the courtyard seemed sturdy enough, although their edges were jagged with age. But with a few coats of varnish we felt they would be much more appropriate than new ones. We did not plan for closets. I had my heart set on furnishing the bedrooms with the towering armoires that seem to hold the soul of Provence. Gilec Aymard understood everything. Vigorous and intelligent, honesty shone from his emerald-flecked eyes. His blunt orange-fuzzed hands were the hands of an artisan who could work, as the French say, like a Benedictine. If he promised doors to lock, windows to open, shutters to shut, and beams without ants, we would have them.

"Could we possibly plan to spend Christmas here?" I asked in a surge of hope, somehow dreaming that Robert, by some stroke of wizardry, could slap up the house in no time.

Building the Ark

Robert looked darkly grave and authoritative as he pondered my impulsive question before answering unexpectedly, "The main wing, yes, madame. My masons will be ready to start the first week in September. But you cannot live here without light and water."

Séguret had a master plumber and electrician in Monsieur Pierre Bonell. He had prospered by installing modern bathrooms and kitchens in the houses of the more forward-looking villagers, including the Faravels. At that time, the Faravels were among the few country people who dared offer their guests the facilities of the house. Most farmers and their families made do with the traditional outhouse in the garden. It was reasoned, and quite rightly so, that any newfangled gadgets first went to adorn the kitchen, as that is where the family spent most of the time, cooking, eating, and entertaining friends over a goblet of wine. Strangers were not expected to go to the bathroom. It was, in fact, considered extremely bad taste to suggest such a thing. Most farms produced far more wine than water. Wine flowed copiously, but water trickled from a meager well, sufficiently full in winter but dangerously low in summer.

Monsieur Bonell came up to see us. A wiry, balding man, in a white undershirt and khaki work pants, he spoke in precise French but with a distinct Spanish accent. An Andorran who had married a local girl and settled in Séguret, Monsieur Bonell looked at us disconcertingly with one eye going east and one eye going west. We showed him where we wanted the bathrooms, one in the guest house, and two in the main house.

"Three water closets and no water?" Monsieur Bonell was flabbergasted.

"Three as a beginning," I said and suggested that all the fixtures in each be installed in one room, the basin, bidet, shower, and toilet. As a concession to the lack of water, I decided in favor of showers instead of bathtubs.

Monsieur Bonell protested at having the toilet in the bathroom. "You must," he said, "have the cabinets as separate rooms."

"That is true if you have only one. But we plan to have at least one bath for every two rooms. I think it is more sensible to have several small bathrooms than one big one and cabinets apart."

"It is against the law." Monsieur Bonell reminded us that French building regulations require the water closet to be accessible at all times. If—*quelle horreur!*—it was to be incorporated into the bathroom, there must, at least, be two doors.

"All right. Then have two doors opening to a bath in the main house."

Monsieur Bonell thoroughly distrusted this plan, but as a sharp merchant he accepted the idea. Later I heard he reported to the villagers that I was a crazy American who wanted three water closets—"Cette folle d'Américaine avec trois salles d'eaux!"

The electricity seemed just as visionary. No wiring reached to the house. The lines stopped at the Faravel property and it was dubious that they would ever extend to our forsaken hillside.

"Temporary lines can be connected from the Faravel place," Robert said. "At least for this winter, and by next summer the regular current should be in from L'Eléctricité de France at Montélimar."

Good. Monsieur Bonell would get on with the wiring as the rooms were built, find a pump for the well, and fit gutters under the eaves to catch the rain water. It seemed obvious that it would be difficult, but Monsieur Bonell was a canny little Andorran who knew *les ficelles du métier*. It would not do to suggest any new tricks to his trade.

We did not consider central heating at all. No one had it in the countryside and in the August sun it was impossible to imagine that snow could lie a foot deep around the ramparts of La Sérafine.

Monsieur Faravel took us to see the Mayor one evening to discuss plans for our road. Monsieur le Maire lived in the plain in a big house with one wing a cave-in of crumbling stones. We left the car at the gate and walked into a courtyard where a mule stood beside an orange tractor. Baskets of peaches were lined up waiting to be trucked to market.

"The Mayor has large orchards," Monsieur Faravel explained. "He is a progressive, good at improving the Commune, especially the roads, although mine is certainly no example." One reason for Monsieur Faravel's interest in our getting a communal road was that his would automatically benefit too.

"Bonjour, Monsieur le Maire," said Monsieur Faravel, introducing us to the small round man with bright brown eyes. The living room was classically Provençal with rush-seated chairs around a table and a hanging lamp above it. "This is our new neighbor in Séguret," said Monsieur Faravel, "but until he has a road I do not know how we will ever get up to see him."

"A road, naturally, but do sit down. There is something I must show you." We sat down, the Mayor switched off the light, put himself squarely in front of a glaring screen, and laughed delightedly. "La télé, la télé," he said proudly. We sat and watched for about fifteen minutes as the family filed in and stood mesmerized behind us. Obviously the boring subject of installing a road to our property could not compete with this fascinating gadget, the first television set in Séguret. After a whispered conference in the corner with Monsieur Faravel, Paul-Marc suggested to the Mayor that a letter might better explain our request for a road. Clearly pleased with this more formal gesture, the Mayor shook our hands rapidly and turned back to his new toy.

The house was our new toy. We sat with the Faravels under the willow tree in their courtyard and spun dreams of whitewashed walls and dark beams and a glass before the fire at Christmas.

"It will all be done in a flash and for a *bouchée de pain!*" Monsieur Faravel called after us as we waved good-bye and took the road to Paris.

CASTLE OF SAND?

If nature provides the sculpture,
I can learn to be a mason.

[FACTEUR CHEVAL, of his Palais Idéal]

Paris, after Provence, came as a rude shock. Not the city itself, which basked in the calm and shade of late August and was still deliciously empty as Parisians stay on holidays until far into September. The shock was the world.

In Provence, I had been caught in the ebb of memory and the flow of imagination. Everything but the immediate slipped away. I left the newspapers unread and washed the radio reports out of mind. At night when the men discussed politics after dinner, I did the dishes and designed the rooms of our unbuilt house. I did not write, not even letters or post-cards. There was no telephone and the only television we had seen was part of a variety show at the Mayor's house. I had shed the world like a pair of stockings.

But the world had not shed us. In Paris, our world was in crisis, because in actuality we related not to the tight cosmos of a hilltown in Provence but to a wider system of world order, or disorder. The Ministry had been calling. No sooner had we unpacked our bags than we heard that my husband was to be sent to the Congo, which was in turmoil, and the length of his mission was unknown. It could be a week or a month or more.

The day the Air France jet sped off the runway for Africa with my husband aboard, a gray September drizzle fell over Paris. Leaves fell from the chestnut trees in the garden, and the apartment, usually so full of life and movement, was dark and silent. I sat miserably in the gloom of Paris trying to write an article on Morocco for my magazine in New York. The sun and peace of Provence seemed a world away, almost as though it had never been. The next morning a letter arrived from Robert Charrasse. The weather was fine, his crew was ready to start work on the house. There was a bulky list of estimates for cement, for tiles, for bulldozers, for stones, for gravel, and for any number of other materials.

I put my manuscript aside and decided to go over the estimates for rebuilding the house.

The pages were very neat, typed in pale-blue ink, but the technical terms were completely outside my French vocabulary. The measurements were in meters and centimeters. Beside each description of the projected work the estimated cost was listed, but listed in new francs.

It was very difficult. I have no head for figures. Numbers bore me and the franc had changed decimal points. I had got used to converting dollars into old francs: fifty thousand francs equaled more or less one hundred dollars. All of a sudden it changed. Now one thousand new francs translated into two hundred dollars. Shifting the decimal point two ciphers became a real problem. I recognized quite well that President de Gaulle was right. New francs were better. To think continually in thousands and millions of francs is corrupting. One gets the feeling of being a millionaire with no sound foundation. I always felt very rich in France until the General changed the monetary system. Suddenly I felt very poor.

I got out my pocket dictionary *Français-Anglais* to look up the mystifying terms as I came to them. The heading was quite clear: ENTREPRISE GÉNÉRALE DE MACONNERIE, BÉTON, ARMÉ, Robert Charrasse, Séguret (Vaucluse). Although my dictionary noted *béton* as "cement" and *armé* as "weapon," I deduced the meaning to be reinforced concrete. The subheading revealed a description and estimate of the projected work to be done at the farm "Michelons," followed by paragraphs of the construction step by step, or rather the destruction.

The first step was to clear and completely demolish the roof, all two thousand thirty-six square feet of it. The roof was then to be repaved with round tiles, limestone, and *pannes*, which translated as "part of a hammer or pig fat," and *chevrons*, or "military stripes depicting the length of service." Two rows of tiles *soigneusement jointés* and trimmed were to remake the *gênoises*, which my little book called "women of Genoa or a cake made of flour, sugar, eggs, and almonds." The floors came next, fourteen hundred square feet of them to be demolished. Floorboards would be relaid and plastered with "hammer-heads," "pig fat," and "military stripes."

To disentangle the confusion of meters and new francs

and baffling construction terms of the first page took me the better part of the morning. I still did not know what half of it meant and only roof, floors, and a few windows had been accounted for. There were two more tightly typed pages to figure out, but I felt too woolly-minded to tackle them at once. There was nothing I could do about it anyway. The masons were probably already at work building the house on the hill. All we needed was money and in the meantime I could find a dictionary to reassure me that our beautiful flaked tiles were not being *soigneusement jointés* with Genoese ladies and almond cakes.

The sun had broken through the mist so I spent the afternoon browsing among the bookstalls along the quais of the Seine. I found a larger dictionary that was both *Français-Anglais* and *Anglais-Français,* and leafing through a portfolio of old engravings came across an illustrated map of the *département* of the Vaucluse. It was emblazoned with the crest of Avignon, three keys crowned with the papal walls. Banners and green garlands entwined the busts of famous citizens on plinths against Rhône cities and a blue sky. Tightly written statistics, the rushing waters of the Fontaine-de-Vaucluse, and a still life of the riches of the region encircled the map. With the help of a magnifying glass proffered by the bookstall owner, I traced the faint road to Séguret.

"That is where we have a house," I announced triumphantly to the map vendor, who was surprised into a smile by this confidence.

"You are lucky, madame. Here is your Vaucluse," he said rolling up the map.

My identity re-established by this chancy find, I returned to Monsieur Charrasse's *devis descriptif et estimatif* with renewed zeal. The first heading of the second page made it clear that I would not be permitted the worn, rounded stones of the two little stairways. Hundreds of feet of downstairs ceilings would be delicately plastered, and hundreds more feet upstairs. Floors, which had already been demolished and relaid, required the finishing charm of russet Provençal tiles. Bricking up the broken-down partitions, cutting a door through the yard-thick walls, refacing the fireplace, opening the chimney, and flagging the hearth totted up another page.

I would have to consult my new dictionary to probe the meaning of the next lines, which headed a list of thirty-two figures in two columns. Multiplied, equaled, and added up, they arrived at six ciphers. This was very alarming. It added up to far more than the sanguine chunk of bread of Monsieur Faravel. If only Paul-Marc had been there he would have explained it all in a minute. Here was I, who couldn't keep my check stubs straight, cracking my head on a mountain of figures and a foreign language and probably getting everything wrong. There was no rush anyway. Everyone said that people in the Midi worked at a snail's pace and we hadn't a prayer of spending Christmas in Provence. We would be lucky to spend the *next* Christmas in the house.

No sooner had I convinced myself that this enormous effort of demolition and reconstruction would stretch over a long period of time than I received an urgent handwritten letter from Robert Charrasse. It was a concise notation of the work that had been completed at La Sérafine, a complete, and somewhat unwelcome, negation of all rumors of Midi sloth.

First, a road more than twelve feet wide had been bulldozed from the Faravels' to our farmhouse, so that the big truck could get through with enough cement and river sand and gravel to consolidate the north wall. The roof was in the process of being torn off, and the old ceilings had practically disappeared. Monsieur Charrasse then excused himself to have to mention that his finances were in a sorry state and so far our payment had not yet been received. He was well ahead of schedule and was expecting our visit to Séguret as we would be sure to find his work satisfactory.

I was stung with remorse. I pulled out the last page of estimates and the dictionary and resolved to fathom the figures immediately.

By reading that *décrépissage* meant "decrepitate" and *dégarnissage* meant "untrim" or "strip," I realized that this referred to the exterior walls, and the frightening list of numbers applied not to francs, but to the footage to be stripped. In all, it merely added up to a total of something above the sum of ten thousand dollars.

Fortunately a call to the bank confirmed that our check had been sent to Robert Charrasse the day before, as well as a check to Madame Leschi as an option on the property. For a few days I felt vastly relieved until a letter from Madame Leschi arrived. She wrote, somewhat alarmingly, that after four months the deed to the property refused to divulge itself. By some strange quirk, the original document sent years ago to the notary in Sablet remained buried in the files. The Marseilles notary had written to the Sablet notary again but, so far, without result. Madame was desolated and hoped that I would accept her most respectful wishes and hopes for a happy ending to this prolonged affair.

At that time I was very precise about the files on our house. I pulled out the folder marked "Leschi," which contained only one typewritten letter. It stated that I had the honor of confirming my agreement on the acquisition of the property called La Sérafine, or Les Michelons, which Madame Leschi owned in the *département* of the Vaucluse, located in the *commune* of Séguret, on which a construction had been erected, now in a dilapidated condition. The final act of possession would be effected when the authentic deed to the property was signed. Under my signature were the words *bon pour accord,* which Madame Leschi had endorsed in her fine slanting hand.

It was hardly a bill of sale. Just the flimsiest pretext on which we based our sole claim to a pile of stones. The final act of possession appeared to be far in the future, and meantime Robert's trucks were trundling up the hill with stones and mortar for the ten masons who were rebuilding La Sérafine, not for us, but for Madame Leschi if she cared to claim it.

During the nights, the jumble of figures danced around in my head and I would wake up at dawn determined to drive down to Provence to see what was happening. Although I trusted Robert Charrasse, I had only his word to take for the remarkable progress on the house. If it were that far advanced, all the more reason for trying to conclude the sale of the property with the notary in Marseilles. All I had to do was get in the car and go.

The hope that Paul-Marc might return earlier than expected held me back. Also my own cowardice. I dreaded facing the notary, who had been so horrified at our flaunting of the Civil Code by putting the property in my name. In the end I did not go to Séguret. My husband returned from Africa and we planned to go to Provence every weekend.

It was not until late October, however, that we were able to leave Paris and drive down to inspect the first rumblings of stone at La Sérafine. Just before leaving, we received a letter from Monsieur Leschi assuring us that the legal matters were advancing. He had been extremely busy reopening classes at the School for Wayward Girls, and every day meant to leave the necessary documents at the notary's office and get our address, which he had misplaced. Now it was done and he was ready to go with us to sign the papers.

This was the news we had been waiting for. It cleared away all the niggling suspicions that we were building a castle of sand, a frangible fortress that could be swept out of our reach by an unforeseen tide of legalities.

We set off in high spirits. The air was crisp and the Vaucluse in late October had shed its summer gold and hazy blue for a sheen of red and silver. Rains had swollen the Ouvèze River to a rushing torrent that overflowed its graveled banks. The grape-gatherers had stripped the vines leaving them light and straight, their foliage now turned as deep a pink as wine. A muted mistral wind sang in the trees, turning the olive branches to pewter and flipping the leaves of the plane trees like fans in the air. Lights were flickering on in the square when we arrived in Vaison-la-Romaine.

It was too late to go on to Séguret, so we settled into the Fabre town house, which we had all to ourselves, and Paul-Marc telephoned Robert Charrasse to announce our arrival. Robert was delighted. He would alert the Faravels and meet us at the house the following morning. Better, we decided, to see it all with a fresh eye. After five hundred miles on the road it was a pleasure to stroll through the streets of Vaison. Shopwindows on the Grand' Rue blazed with light, the yellow post office was still open, and the tables of the cafés on the Place de Montfort were set up for business. The weather was too fresh for most of the customers who stood inside at the bars having their evening apéritif, but we were so enchanted to breathe the pure air of Provence again that we took a table outside and ordered a glass of wine. One by one the shopkeepers took in their wares off the streets and rolled down their shutters for the night.

When we left to walk through the deserted streets to the Quai Pasteur, the great pits of Roman digs, flowered and floodlit for the summer people, were as black as the mines. Pools of light marked the cafés, the gas stations, and the headlights of an occasional truck lumbering along the Route of the Princes of Orange; otherwise the town was plunged in darkness. The people were in their houses, shuttered and cozy and *en famille*. Gay and festive in summer, Vaison, in autumn and winter, like all provincial places, went to bed early.

The next morning we had breakfast at the Fabres' big kitchen table and left around ten for Séguret. The Faravels must have been listening for the car. Monsieur Faravel stood between his two tall cypress trees beckoning Paul-Marc to stop in his driveway. "Bonjour, bonjour," he said pulling us out of the car as he pumped our hands. "We have been working. Ah, monsieur, how we have been working!" He flung his arms in the direction of the new road. Madame Faravel came out looking thin and cold although the sun had burned the chill off the morning air.

"I will drive you up in my old car," said Monsieur Faravel. "Yours will get stuck. It's pretty rough and the big truck going back and forth all the time has ruined my road. It was bad enough before, but now it's impossible. And the Mayor will do nothing. Nothing."

Monsieur Faravel gave us a running account of the work.

The little hillside used to be so peaceful. Now it was a hive of activity. Hammers banging all day. Masons storming up the path on noisy motorbikes. River sand and odd bricks falling off the truck into his driveway. "It is fortunate," Monsieur Faravel said, "that Madame Faravel and I are early risers or we would have been driven crazy."

We chugged through the ruts and ditches that the bulldozer had carved from the brush, laughing and bouncing and listening to Monsieur Faravel's descriptions of his unflagging efforts on our behalf. Not only had he harvested his grapes and directed the endless flow of traffic, but hardly a day had passed that he had not come up to inspect the work. "Voilà, we are here," he said steering the car into the shade of the cypress trees. "Your Domaine des Michelons."

We walked around the north wall to the east gate where a huge bulbous cement mixer was twirling and grinding out a river of gray ooze. Robert Charrasse came forward to meet us, smiling and tanned. "Bonjour, we are glad to see you. Come on, come inside and see your house now."

The masons turned to stare at us and we shook hands with them, strong, dark-eyed men from the Mediterranean. Señor Angel was laying bricks on the chimney piece around a heavy beam that formed the mantel. He was shy and handsome and touchingly young to be doing such hard manual work. The others were burlier and hardened to the raw, dank air that emanates from half-built houses. They joked and laughed while they hammered and plastered, but Angel was grave and his hands were as soft as a student's. I wanted to know more about him, this boy who looked like a prince but had come to France to work as a common laborer. When I admired his skill and asked where he had learned his trade, he said, "In

Castle of Sand?

Spain, madame, I was an apprentice at fourteen, but here I am paid like an artist." It was clear that Robert's men liked him and worked well for him.

"Allez, allez, look at your house." Monsieur Faravel took me into the cave where Robert and Paul-Marc were inspecting the walls. Sad gray blotches of dampness showed through and, as Robert predicted, they would need more coats of cement and plaster. Upstairs the rooms looked like a cell block, all an ashen color ready to be plastered white. Neither beams, nor windows, nor doors had been installed to add a softening stroke of wood to the bareness. The cement floors awaited their rich shine of tiles; the gaping holes, their protective panels of glass. I had expected much more, but the lines were drawn, the rooms defined. There were the three bedrooms, each with its small flight of flagstone steps leading to a high doorway. Monsieur Bonnell would come in later with his electrical wiring and plumbing fixtures. Monsieur Aymard had already measured for the jambs, and sills, and shutters. The little room off the east staircase looked almost livable because of the old olivewood banister and the worn red tiles that had been left intact.

Knowing my preference for the old stones of the stairwells, Robert had replaced them with weathered slabs that seemed more ancient than they were. In the room where the cistern dripped, he had shown a superior sense of design by keeping part of the thick wall and converting it into a stony bar. Outside, scaffolding and ladders framed the walls which the masons were smoothing and cementing. No patches of old stone would show through, as I had hoped, as Robert assured us that only their density had kept the walls from falling like a house of cards.

"But it is an old house, I want it to look that way, not as though it had been built yesterday," I pleaded.

"I will prove to you how old it is. Follow me," said Robert climbing up a ladder to the roof. Paul-Marc went up after him and they urged me to follow. We crawled over the slanting surface to the brick chimney hooded in tiles. Under the shelter of the hood so that the wind and rain would not efface its history, Robert had placed a flaxen tile, seemingly more scratched than the others. "Look at it," he said. "Read the date carved into it." We squinted down at the scrolled numbers and made out the date—1648.

This was a great discovery. The first actual knowledge we had of the place reaching further back into time than Monsieur Faravel's childhood memories. "Now you know why there is so much work to be done here," Robert said. "The house probably has not been touched since then, except for the pavilion my father added on to the west wing for the Leschis."

"The Leschis!" exclaimed Monsieur Faravel. "I have heard nothing from them. Did you ever receive the papers for the house?"

"We must go to Marseilles this afternoon and sign the bill of sale," Paul-Marc explained.

"Come and have a glass of wine with us first. These Parisians, always in a hurry. We wanted you to stay for lunch. Madame Faravel will be very disappointed." Monsieur Faravel shook his head and shrugged in disgust. In Provence it is considered very bad manners to breeze in and out without stopping long enough for a conversation and a meal. So we did stay for lunch after all, later racing to Marseilles to meet Monsieur Leschi and his mother at the ap-

pointed hour of five at the notary's office. A folder of papers
was brought in and Madame Leschi and I signed sheet after
sheet of typewritten pages. Each one had to be stamped and
sealed and witnessed. Totally baffled by these legalities, I
looked to Paul-Marc for approval and he nodded before I
wrote my signature on each document. Then we handed
over the check for the final amount due and received one
sheet of paper and a receipt. This, the notary informed us,
was the bill of sale. The deed to the property had been located but was not yet in his hands. As soon as he received it
from the notary in Sablet, all necessary legal steps would be
taken and the final documents sent to us. Meantime, we could
consider ourselves the owners of the Domaine des Michelons or La Sérafine, however we wished to call it. He obviously considered either name a pretentious title for the
worthless hillside we laid claim to in the Vaucluse. His fee
had been paid, but all things considered, it had been a great
deal of bother and a financial disaster for the notary, and one
not yet finished with at that. He herded us all out of his office with a distraught sigh of relief.

Now, for the first time since June we could leave Séguret
and go back to Paris with the proof that the property was
actually ours. Any walls that had to be wrecked and rewrought
would be for our own house. Finally, after five months, the
earth and the stones of La Sérafine belonged to us, although
in fact, of the stack of mystifying pages I had signed, we still
had only a scrap of paper to show for it.

COLD CHRISTMAS
IN PROVENCE

Nature still feeds her children . . .
her cruel breast will always yield
sweet oil to the olive tree.

[MISTRAL, *Calendal*]

I have always found that the mills of the gods grind not
slowly but with alarming jolts, fragmenting the landscape of
existence into unpredictable patterns. No sooner had we
mapped a serene spring and summer of moving between Paris
and Provence to watch La Sérafine stretch and grow than
the cataclysm came. My husband was to be seconded from
the Ministry of Foreign Affairs in Paris to the United Nations in New York. We were due to leave the first week in
January of the new year.

Cold Christmas in Provence

The plans for a Christmas holiday in Provence took on the dimensions of obsession, as it was to be our last glimpse of La Sérafine for months to come. An ocean would separate us from the vine and the rock of the Vaucluse. Paul-Marc's children, Jacques and Nicole, longed to see their farmhouse in Provence and we couldn't wait to show it to them. From all accounts the house sounded inviting, if not quite a paragon of comfort. Madame Faravel, who always did the writing for Monsieur Faravel, informed us that a well digger had been found to rid the well of its infected source of débris and deepen it by a meter. Monsieur Bonell's one bath, pipes, wiring, and drains—all carefully notated in his neat, spidery handwriting—were in the process of being installed. Monsieur Aymard's doors and windows were promised. We glowed in the reflection of Madame Faravel's rosy prose: the weather was superb . . . Monsieur Bonell's work was both solid and' soigné . . . if the well always remained so full, life would be marvelous. A postscript assured us that the baker who owned the depot of Séguret had announced the arrival of our beds from Paris. The baker's letter, however, hardly echoed the rosiness of Madame Faravel's.

"Chère Madame, cher Monsieur," he wrote. "The furniture which you sent to our depot arrived safely and we carted it up the hill by tractor as Monsieur Charrasse could not be bothered. Naturally we are delighted that you will come for Christmas but having remarked the intense dampness of your house, we feel you will find it uninhabitable. Not only are the windows open to the sky, but the tiles are far from laid. The well is full of water but there is no electricity. The road is impassable. We look forward to seeing you with great pleasure and please accept our deep friendship."

We set off in a spirit of high adventure hardly knowing what to expect. Nicole, a round and beautiful fourteen, wore a fur bonnet and boots with a green coat that matched her oyster-green eyes. Jacqui, as dark-eyed and slight as a Greek shepherd boy, dressed in ski clothes. At fifteen he was an excellent athlete, used to spending winter vacations on the ski slopes of the Haute-Savoie and summers scuba diving in the Mediterranean. I wondered how these two charming, protected young people would react to the rigors of our faraway hillside in Provence. It was Christmas Eve and I was warmed by my Christmas present from Paul-Marc, a fluffy black poodle puppy that, to the consternation of the French, I named Bête-Noire.

We arrived at our bend of the road at dusk. The baker had not exaggerated. The ruts and ditches were impassable. The wheels spun in their tracks and no amount of backing and filling, no shifting of gears or pushing would induce the car to budge. There was nothing to do but leave it and start climbing. Long blue shadows darkened the woods. With suitcases, cartons of food, and utensils dangling, we took to the road on foot. Not a light shone in the windows of the Faravel house as we trudged by. We struggled to keep up with Paul-Marc striding ahead, the baggage strapped across his shoulders like a porter in the Gare de Lyon. " 'Allons enfants . . . le jour de gloire est arrivé . . .' " he sang back, rousing our wilting exhilaration. Only the absurd delight of the little poodle kept us going. We slaked off our jagged tempers by scolding her for prancing through the dark forest instead of letting ourselves cavil against the cold. Mindlessly, she ran to the crest of the last hill and began to bark. We heard voices and as we reached the rise we saw Monsieur and Madame Faravel.

Cold Christmas in Provence

"Soyez les bienvenus, soyez les bienvenus," they called, smiling, their arms outspread in wide embrace.

We staggered through the courtyard and into the house. Lights glowed. A fire blazed in the chimney. A bottle of wine and six goblets shone on a card table spread with a green linen cloth. In one corner stood a stiff spruce tree hung with red and gold Christmas balls. From the scarred beam of the olive press a white taffeta ribbon unfurled its greeting: *Joyeux Noël.*

"The tree is from your land, the wine from mine. To your first night at La Sérafine!" Monsieur Faravel filled the glasses and the warmth of our spirits cast off the chill of the night.

Madame Faravel told us that Madame Fabre had scaled the icy hill that afternoon with the Christmas decorations and left a note inviting us for Christmas dinner the following day. The Faravels expected us that night for *réveillon,* the Christmas Eve dinner, after the midnight Mass in the Church of Saint-Denis in Séguret. Long famous throughout the countryside, Mass of the Shepherds was sung in Provençal. Everyone in the village was taking part, a spectacular occasion as this Christmas Eve was the first time it had been performed in twenty-nine years.

Overwhelmed by our reception and revived by the warming wine, we set about arranging the house. Actually there was very little to arrange, no tables or chairs, or chests or armoires, just the beds to be made and the kitchen stuff stored away. We stripped the beds of their burlap coverings, which Jacqui sanely suggested we use as rugs. The glow of the downstairs fire hardly penetrated to the upstairs rooms, which were as glacial as a deep freeze. We battened down the shutters to stave off the wind and lit the butane-gas stoves ordered from Monsieur Bonell. I searched desperately for the light sockets to plug in the short-corded lamps. Where were they? Scrambling around the frigid tiles I aimed a flashlight at the floorboards along the walls, but to no avail. "Where are the prises d'électricité?" I called down frantically to Monsieur Faravel. He scampered up the stone steps and found them right away in the furthest corner of each long dark room. "You did not want overhead lighting in the Provençal way, so Monsieur Bonell put a socket in each room à l'Américaine," said Monsieur Faravel, plugging in the black wrought-iron lamp which splayed like a spider in its pool of light, leaving the rest of the hayloft in eerie darkness. Melted snow seemed to run from the taps in the one frosty bathroom as Monsieur Faravel explained that the hot-water heater had not yet arrived.

"A disaster," Madame Faravel advised as I shiveringly stacked the dishes and utensils in the moldy back kitchen where Monsieur Bonell had installed the stainless-steel sink at knee level and connected a dirty-gray secondhand two-burner stove to a mammoth bottle of butane gas. I steamed inwardly. America and Andorra would never see eye to eye on the thorny issues of bathrooms and kitchens and electric sockets.

"What a miracle. For the first time in history there is light in this farmhouse. Did you see the cable that Monsieur Bonell strung through the trees from our house?" Monsieur Faravel's sudden reminder of the enormous effort to make La Sérafine livable gave me pangs of guilt. "We finished laying the tiles and fitting the windows yesterday just before Robert Charrasse went off to hunt in Alsace for the holidays."

"But his father, Monsieur André Charrasse, and his sister, Josette, are taking part in the Shepherds' Mass. It begins at ten; we must be going now if we want to find seats in the church."

We bundled into our coats and trotted down the hill as though we were going to a party, all of us filled with unspoken joy at not having to spend the evening huddled by the meager fire in our bleak farmhouse. Streams of cars curled up the road to Séguret. We left our cars in the square of the Place de la Bise and joined the pilgrims filing through the narrow lane of the rue du Château Fort. Séguret had never been so lively. Water spouted from the lips of the four masked heads of the Fontaine des Mascarons facing the Mairie. Lights flooded the steep cobbled steps leading to Saint-Denis, the Romanesque church that had hovered protectively over the village since the tenth century. Every *prie-Dieu* was taken when we arrived and people spilled outside, standing on chairs for a better view through the opened portals. The organ boomed. I squeezed through the entrance for a look at the magnificent *Crèche-Vivante:* the Madonna, St. Joseph, the Christ Child in a manger surrounded by shepherds with live lambs on their shoulders. "There's Monsieur André Charrasse." Monsieur Faravel pointed out a woodcutter in a long blue tunic and brown velvet trousers with a crook and a sack on his back. "There is Josette." Madame Faravel all but waved to a trembling angel in gauzy white, her golden halo wobbling in the icy breeze. The *Crèche-Vivante* intoned the Mass in Provençal, while the chorus answered in French. "Fifty villagers take part. It is a very old Mass that lasts two hours," Monsieur Faravel whispered loudly. The Faravels recognized all their friends. "The grocer, Monsieur Paris, is St. Joseph. The baker is one of the Three Kings. The postman, Monsieur Giely, is a woodcutter. Monsieur Henri

Martin is playing the organ." The actors were dressed warmly in costumes designed like those of the seventy-two traditional *santons,* the wood-carved figurines that form the *crèche* of the famous Provençal Christmas story. We were congealed, rubbing our elbows and stamping our feet to keep them from going numb. Madame Faravel's nose had turned pink with cold, but she weathered the spectacle for an hour before suggesting we return for the feast of the *réveillon.*

The Faravels' kitchen was an oasis of delicious scents and warmth. A soup of lasagna shivered on the stove and we spooned it into deep bowls. Monsieur Faravel poured his strongest, most bracing red wine. Then we had spinach with coarse country ham before the traditional codfish with a dry white wine. Cheeses were passed, and afterwards, *la panado,* an apple tart served especially on Christmas Eve. Such abundance. We were overwhelmed. I was beginning to realize that this good country life was an enormous accomplishment, well thought out and supported by a system of long-term planning. I had a hollow feeling that no amount of effort on my part could ever make me a match for the superior talents of Madame Faravel. I was overcome with gratitude to be spending Christmas Eve in her kitchen and not in my own.

We thanked the Faravels profusely and started home. Home—it was hardly the word for the cold rooms and clammy beds that awaited us after we trudged up the moon-flooded path to the top of the hill. Paul-Marc lit the fire and put a bottle of champagne and some glasses on the card table. We were all exhausted. It was one in the morning. But no matter how cold or how exhausted we were this was *réveillon,* Christmas Eve. *Il faut des rites.* This in France is the traditional moment for the opening of Christmas presents. Paul-

Marc plugged in the tree lights and Jacqui and Nicole warmed their hands by the fire. I climbed up the dark stairs to our room to find the presents.

"Mes enfants, à La Sérafine," said Paul-Marc ceremoniously, handling us each a glass. "Joyeux Noël." We clinked glasses, forced by his buoyancy out of our apathy. "This is my Christmas present," I said, picking up Bête-Noire, holding her warm shaggy body next to mine. "Here is yours, Nicole." She took off her woolen mittens and untied with stiff fingers the green bow, immediately recognizing the gray-and-white box from Dior. Inside she found a pair of long satin gloves. It was the most absurd Christmas present imaginable at La Sérafine. We all laughed. Jacqui had a Sony transistor radio which he tuned in. Paul-Marc found his gold cuff links the silliest things in the world. The only presents that made any sense were the warm cashmere sweaters Paul-Marc had bought the children in England. They put them on instantly and woke up in them the next morning.

Christmas morning: the sun shone as brightly as the moon had shone the night before. We were learning to live with our burlap carpets and the icy water stinging our faces and the way the toothpaste seemed to turn to snow as we brushed our teeth. Still, my puritan conscience hurt at the lack of a warm bath. I put on pots of water to boil and hauled them upstairs, one each for Jacques, Nicole, and myself, leaving Paul-Marc to sing his way valiantly through his cold shower. We rolled one of the butane stoves into the frigid bathroom, spread bath towels on the floor, and one by one, sponged down.

It was a gala day. Christmas—and Roger and Régine expected us for the holiday dinner.

We put on the few good clothes we had brought. To me, it

felt wonderful to get out of boots and pants, to make up carefully, and feel the pinch of gold earrings. I wonder if I am really cut out for the country life? I asked myself. But then I was the one who had found the house and insisted on having it. This was not the day to feel remorse, much less show it. Bête-Noire was standing on the bed wagging her tail in complete disagreement. We dashed down the stone steps ready for the trek down to the car. The sky was so blue, the air so clear, the ground so firm, that my churlish mood vanished into the sunlit sky.

Régine met us at the door in a green dress, the exact color of her ravishing eyes. The boys fell on the poodle puppy, finding her far more interesting than the presents we had brought them. We went into the drawing room, where a fire blazed in the chimney and the tall windows were half-shuttered to the light. Even in winter, the sun remained the enduring enemy of Régine's petit-point chairs and Aubusson rugs.

In the dining room, the table gleamed in silver and crystal on the white damask cloth. Red roses struck by candlelight flowered as a centerpiece surrounded by place settings of family silver and Limoges porcelain. Stemmed glasses stood at each place, and a sprig of holly adorned each napkin wrapped around a roll. We all exclaimed that it was *ravissant* as Régine seated us, separating the two families except for Jean-Charles, who sat next to his mother. At five, he ate everything the adults ate.

Roger presided over the table, a genial, charming host, smiling his joy at our having joined their Provençal world. He lifted his glass to toast us, old friends and new neighbors. The maid went round the table, silently, endlessly, serving each dish twice, changing the plates for each course. Régine re-spected every formality. No matter what the effort or the un-remitting energy and grace required to serve nine people at the long table, she would permit no shortcuts. The meal went on for hours, long delicious hours of tasting a variety of dishes, of sipping cool Chablis and heady Châteauneuf-du-Pape.

The desserts were brought in, an array of tarts, the tradi-tional *bûche de Noël,* a bowl of raspberry ice, silver-wrapped *marrons glacés,* and a great wooden tray of nuts and fruits. "Treize, treize," the children screamed, delighted to indulge in the Provençal rite of having thirteen desserts at Christmas. "Doucement," quieted Régine. "Each one may have thirteen different things, but remember to count everything, a nut counts for one dessert, or a grape." The children filled their plates gleefully as Roger popped the champagne cork. Even Jean-Charles, by now quite flushed and sleepy, was allowed a soupçon of champagne. "Joyeux Noël, may we have many in Provence together!" We all clinked glasses, aflame with sentiment and the fire of the grape.

"You must have lunch with us tomorrow at La Sérafine," Paul-Marc insisted expansively. Jacques and Nicole echoed the invitation: "You must come, we will have a pique-nique." I sobered at the thought, but the Fabres' feast had been so de-licious, so full of heartfelt warmth and friendship, that it would have been impossibly gauche not to reciprocate, no matter how meager our efforts might seem in comparison.

The next morning I counted knives and forks, plates and glasses, and no matter how many times I went through the equipment, the number came dismally to four each.

"Couldn't we have an apéritif here and take them for lunch in Vaison-la-Romaine?" I asked Paul-Marc in desperation. "Quelle blague! We have invited the Fabres to our house, and to our house they will come," he answered firmly.

"In that case, Jacques's idea of a pique-nique is not bad. Why don't we have an American picnic, a barbecue in the courtyard with grilled hamburgers?" It was the twenty-sixth of December but the sun shone hot and the mistral blew not a whisper. To me, this seemed a splendid solution.

"Hamburgers? Have you lost your mind? That is not food!" I pointed to the depressing selection of pots and pans stacked against the damp kitchen wall. "There are limits, really. I simply don't think I can cope with it."

"I assure you it will be excellent," Paul-Marc insisted.

"Excellent? After the fantastic lunch the Fabres gave us yesterday? It will be embarrassing. What will Régine think? Her perfection as a maîtresse de maison fills me with complexes as it is!"

"I will take everything in charge," he added confidently. "Come on, let's go to Orange and see what we can find there."

Orange rumbled with traffic. We inched through the narrow streets until we came to a square with the Hôtel de Ville on one side and a *Prisunic* supermarket on the other. I found some pretty Italian plates, black-handled knives and forks, and the kind of wineglasses used in street cafés. After I bought a red linen tablecloth and napkins, my sagging morale took a great leap forward. I let Paul-Marc cope with the food, which he did in dark secrecy for fear I might descend to the ignominy of chopped *bifteck*. We met at a table in the glass-enclosed café where Jacques and Nicole waited with Bête-Noire, and had a shell of beer before heading back for La Sérafine far more jubilant than when we had left.

By the time we returned the courtyard had been warmed

to the temperature of a solarium so we decided to eat out-of-doors. We put the card table and four chairs in a protected corner near the stable and Jacques cleared a patch of the terrace and stretched a few planks across stones to make a picnic board. Spread with the new red cloth, set with the cutlery, and flanked by the folding chairs with red cushions, our luncheon table looked delightfully gay and colorful. Nicole arranged the picnic board with straw mats, napkins, glasses, knives, and forks. It was rough, but rustic. Hardly a *fête-champêtre*, but at least a *déjeuner* not quite *sur l'herbe*. A proper French picnic with everyone seated for the usual four courses you might have in any normal French dining room. The thought of sandwiches with paper napkins, or wine served in waxed cups, or people lounging about munching hard-boiled eggs, is to the French unthinkable, as odd to them as we find their simmering a *coq-au-vin* for a picnic.

We heard the wheels of the car on the road and went running out to greet the Fabres. They had navigated the rocky climb in their springy 2 CV and arrived en masse at the west entrance to the house. Roger laughed delightedly when he saw the courtyard set for a *pique-nique* and said this was the true Provence, lunch in the sunlight of December. For the boys it was great fun to be in the wild country, out of a house too beautiful to romp and play in. We shed our coats and had a Dubonnet in the warm corner while Paul-Marc disappeared into the kitchen to fix his mysterious dish.

I could not imagine what he had undertaken for so many people until he emerged triumphantly carrying a large glazed earthenware pot. We all exclaimed with the expected praise as he lifted the lid with a flourish to reveal a bubbly version of the famous Alsatian *choucroute garnie*. Jacques drew the corks, Nicole passed the bread, and I ladled out the steamy sausages and ham and sauerkraut in the casserole. It was a huge success. There was no need to feel the slightest complex of inferiority about the hospitality of La Sérafine. For a moment we were tempted to stay on to ring in the new year, but, in the end, common sense prevailed and we decided to forsake the pioneering life of Provence for the comforts of Paris.

A light snow powdered the path as we trekked down to the car with our suitcases in the morning. We stopped to say good-bye to Monsieur and Madame Faravel, wishing them a *bonne année,* before taking the road. Paul-Marc drove through the valley so that he could see the house in the distance, looking immense and white on the green hillside. He gave it a long, lingering, loving glance. His passion for La Sérafine had risen in ratio to my doubts. He and the children looked hale and tanned, but I was feeling pale and squeamish. My limitations of domesticity had been sorely tried. Even under ideal conditions, it is a supreme challenge to be a paragon French wife, but in a half-built house with Monsieur Bonell's elusive light sockets, glacial water, and a stainless-steel sink installed at knee level, it was all but impossible. I was again aware that the complications of French civilization must be met at all costs. No quarter is given for lack of equipment or a two-burner stove. After all, the most extraordinary cuisine in the world was created on woodburning stoves and with no hot water at all.

"It was a wonderful pique-nique yesterday. The Fabres loved La Sérafine," Paul-Marc said, his thoughts so completely contradicting my own that I had to laugh. He was right. It had been a wonderful picnic, one that we would all remember for the rest of our lives.

EXPLOSION
OF A MYTH

*A wee house
has a wide throat.*

[SCOTTISH PROVERB]

Blizzards swirled about New York and we were well settled into a twentieth-floor penthouse by the time the final deed to La Sérafine arrived from the notary in Marseilles. An impressive document of eight closely typewritten pages stamped and sealed with the imprint of Marianne de France, it filled us with pride of ownership. It also gave us the exact dimensions of our land and a fascinating history of the previous owners, which, with a certain spiteful delight aimed at the distant notary, I discovered to be women.

The document detailed the dates of marriage of the owners,

their legal status, and the fact that they had all been protected from the Code Napoléon by a contract of marriage that guaranteed their dotal rights to the property along with their paraphernalia. Quite a triumph for these provincial girls, I thought, considering that the negotiations reached back to the early nineteenth century.

After close scanning, I realized that we were the owners of a territory in the Commune of Séguret (Vaucluse), in the region of the Jas, of the Esclade, and of Mont Vert, composed of a pavilion with vineyards, fields, and olive groves. It all added up to about six hectares, or a little over twelve acres. In accepting the property we were responsible for the deplorable condition of the buildings without the right to reclaim redress from the former owner. We would take all risks and perils, and pay all expenses, legal and otherwise, and assume the taxes so that the vendor would never suffer inquietude or be bothered by this subject. I was only too pleased to take the responsibility, recalling the tons of cement and the hours of labor that had been poured into the farmhouse months before it had been actually ours.

Entrée en Possession/Jouissance, the legal term for full ownership, created multiple joys in the true meanings of the French words. With double force, it translated as extreme pleasure derived from possession, and an action in which one's capital has been reimbursed and in which no other shall receive the benefits accrued therefrom.

Like many Americans, I harbored a fond and false fantasy that dollars stretch further on foreign soil. Any property or labor costs were bound to be half of what they were at home. The happy villagers, especially those of the Mediterranean countries, would automatically lend their skills and time, the materials would be hewn from native stone and wood, and haphazardly an indigenous, timeless dwelling would emerge for a fraction of what it would cost in Connecticut or Virginia. The Vaucluse, to me, symbolized the fulfillment of this illusion. Too far inland from the Riviera to attract yachting millionaires, too rural for industry, too remote and inherently French for non-French-speaking visitors, it held the *luxe, calme et volupté* of faraway places, the *ordre et beauté* of uncorrupted innocence. In stumbling on to Séguret, I thought I had found an oasis bypassed by the caravans of trade.

Bit by bit the myth exploded, set off first by the sequence of detonations of the Charrasse estimates and followed in close succession by those of Monsieur Bonell. These we accepted with exalted equanimity, realizing we had been lulled into a trance of delightful delusion by Monsieur Faravel's rapt and erroneous appraisals.

On our last visit to Provence, Robert Charrasse had brought in his friend from the Société Marseillaise de Crédit in Vaison-la-Romaine. Having channeled all our payments through his branch of the bank we felt, by now, that we deserved an excellent credit rating. We had greeted the young banker with due formality, chatting sociably and offering him a *pastis* in the living room before raising the prickly matter of money. The neat little man in his dark suit asked a few pointed questions sounding out my husband as to his diplomatic status and general financial standing, which Robert assured him was as sound as the Louis. All to the good, but my husband had hoped to offer as collateral the main wing of the house—a solid structure that, as far as we were concerned, was paved in gold. With proper discretion we showed him around the rooms. He nodded approvingly, raising our hopes, and Robert prodded his memory by repeating the millions of *anciens francs* that had poured from our banks to his. Everything went beautifully until we reached the dining room. "What is this?" asked the sober banker, tapping the thick stone wall that Robert had sensibly smoothed and retained from the ancient cistern. Two feet wide and about five feet long, it cut through the room and served as a catch-all and serving table for the casseroles passed from the kitchen to the dining room.

"This is a bar. A maison de luxe!" exclaimed the banker. "Un signe extérieur de richesse . . . an overt sign of wealth. Why should you have credit?" At that time, the French, notoriously secretive and frugal about money, were taxed on exterior signs of wealth, affluence obvious to the eye of the taxman, who doubtlessly suspected masses of gold hoarded in the wine cellar—such as a car, a swimming pool, a country house, and, we gathered, especially a country house with a bar.

"The bar was mere accident. I designed it on the spur of the moment. Monsieur did not even ask for it," Robert assured him.

"A maison de luxe?" Paul-Marc's voice rose angrily. "This is a humble peasant's farmhouse that we are trying, at great effort, to make habitable. Dying land that we want to bring to life. A forgotten village into which we are injecting new hope. What do you mean an overt sign of wealth?"

This heated response got the credit man's back up. "If we should decide to grant you credit, monsieur, exactly where would the money come from and in what currency?" the banker asked testily.

"It would come from my bank in New York and in dollars," Paul-Marc answered.

"Dollars? Not in French francs? That is serious. We do not like currency of foreign countries." The banker, an unreconstructed provincial, was plainly out of his depth in any but local terms.

"You do not like dollars? What about the Marshall Plan, monsieur?" Paul-Marc went on to expound the long history of Franco-American relations, but to no avail. The banker had shaken hands coldly and departed without having understood a word, more firmly opposed to our cause than ever.

Sadder but wiser, we had accepted this rebuff philosophically. At least we were sprung from the trap of being in hock for years at the high interest rates of French banks. It would have to be pay-as-you-go, and agonizing as it might be in the process, eventually La Sérafine would be all ours with no strings attached.

We were in constant touch with Robert Charrasse about the next slice of work to be done on the house. Not only was the little house in the courtyard to be finished but the terrace. "The house will slide off its rock ledge and into the valley if the retaining wall is not reinforced," Robert had written, and we had answered, of course, to fix the wall. In order to continue the work of the Domaine des Michelons in the Quartier Saint-Jean, a Devis Estimatif from the Aménagement de l'Habitat Rural would need shaping up, along with an architect's plan for the future house as it would be. La Sérafine was becoming a house by correspondence course. Paul-Marc wrote yes to everything. There was nothing else we could do. Régine Fabre could spend the spring months between Paris and Provence, cosseting and forming Chanteduc to her own mold. When the workmen came, she would be up at dawn bouncing up the mountain in her small car to smile and charm the masons into placing every stone where she wanted it. No window would be cut, no tile laid without her clear green eye upon it. I, on the other hand, could only imagine the progress of the series of new rooms we planned for La Sérafine. We placed our trust in the judgment and style of Robert Charrasse and dreamed of spending summer holidays in the house.

We roughed out a floor plan of how we more or less envisioned the unfinished wings and sent it off to Robert: two bedrooms and a bath in the guest house; a two-story beamed living room with a gallery in the stable; a laundry, maid's room, and garage in the west pavilion. The center of gravity of any house changes as it grows, just as original plans expand and the planes of space reorient to different forms. At the beginning our ideas crowded around the fireplace of the living room where we had huddled for warmth at Christmastime. Winter thoughts inspired Paul-Marc to think of sheltering the car. The dank scullery and the glacial picnic for nine motivated my conceit to house that phantasmagoric village girl, *la bonne à tout faire*. In summer, when the world of Provence opened to the sun and sky and fresh breezes swept away the winter shadows, we would change our floor plan to reach out and embrace the west wing, pulling it into the main body as another unit of living. We would start now with the terrace and the guest house and leave the west wing for later, and meantime the authorities could draw up their full estimate from this plan.

This being done, we sank into a torpor of complacency, convinced that the main wing had been the costliest and any further expenses would be as easy to swing as a basket of salad. A beautiful architectural floor plan arrived, making La Sérafine seem a mansion on the drafting board. Heights of ceilings and lengths of walls were marked. Seven different levels of roofs cut across the façade. Fifteen staircases, inside and out, ranging from two to ten marches rose and fell to the rooms. Doors swung, windows opened, and a neat wooden railing spanned the staircase leading to the gallery in the living room.

"It is not a *mas* but a *manoir!*" I exclaimed, overcome by the opulence of the plan.

"They seem to think we are building a château," Paul-Marc remarked dryly, noting the price tag from the Fédération Nationale des Bureaux d'Études et Techniciens en Batiments in L'Isle-sur-la-Sorgue. "This looks like one of our United Nations project reports," he said opening the fifty-page list of estimates for the reincarnation of the terrace, rabbit warrens, dovecote, stable, and pavilion. Every stroke of the paintbrush for two or three coats was described, every hum of the saw for beams, every washer on Monsieur Bonell's copper pipes, every nail hammered into Monsieur Aymard's door jambs, every ounce of demolition and reconstruction to be rendered by the squad of Spanish masons under the supervision of Robert Charrasse. Delving back to the beginnings, the report scanned the work already accomplished and "based on the known economic values of the day" foretold the work of the future.

It was a most impressive document, but most impressive of all was the final figure on the fiftieth page. Twenty-five thousand dollars. And that, as it turned out, was just the beginning.

Snow flurries and winter winds delayed any further work on the house until spring, Robert wrote, adding nonchalantly that any bank credit still was as elusive as a butterfly. We liquidated some blue-chip stocks and I happily rejoined my colleagues on the magazine. Our pile of stones was lengthening from a *bouchée de pain* to a *bâtard*.

A VINEYARD FOR
LA SÉRAFINE

*Le vin est la plus saine
et la plus hygiénique des boissons.*

[LOUIS PASTEUR]

Paul-Marc wanted a vineyard more than anything in the world. For him, like most Frenchmen, wine is a way of life, a persuasive civilizing factor in human relations, a cohesive element in the *savoir-vivre* of France. His family had never sat down to the table without well-selected vintages, sniffed, sipped, discussed, and most of all, enjoyed with shameless zest. As an American I had been brought up in a family aware of good wines. Wine had always been part of an occasion. The magnum of Dom Pérignon for Christmas, a few bottles of Chambertin or Montrachet at Thanksgiving or Easter, but wine, except for the few years we lived in Europe,

A Vineyard for La Sérafine

had not been an everyday blessing. Wine for us was a celebration, each bottle poured from its basket and drunk with solemnity bordering on reverence.

When I went to live in France, I was astonished to hear the French proclaiming wine as merely "respectable," "passable," or "drinkable," and consuming it in far greater degree than water. In Paris, the flow of spirits at our table ranged from the richest Burgundies to the meanest *ordinaires*. And the flow was endless. The only thing that outranked quality was quantity and I soon realized that the one unforgivable sin for a hostess would be to reach the dregs of the keg.

There was always the dinner for the "great" wines, but for everyday, the "little" wines were perfectly acceptable and, in fact, preferred. It was a triumph to come up with a special *petit vin* rather than a known *grand cru*. A French gallantry says, *où l'hôtesse est belle, le vin est bon,* and if where the hostess is beautiful, the wine is good, I often felt that the real *veritas* was in the *vino:* the more the wine, the better the hostess. What bliss to have our own vineyard in the Vaucluse, our own label, our own infinite cellar never to run dry.

More than a whim, it seemed a historical necessity. Our property stood in the heart of the Rhône Valley, which for over two thousand years had yielded a sea of wine. The Greeks and Romans planted the first rootstocks on the steep limestone slopes of the hundred-and-forty-mile vertebrae stretching from Lyons to Avignon. Hard by the river Rhône, the French popes cultivated vineyards and swooned over the pungent, manly wines of their summer seat at Châteauneuf-du-Pape. Through the ages, wine had been the sustenance and security, the pride and pleasure, the art and the craft of all the princes, poets, and peasants of Provence.

Our peasants' *mas,* by now fleshed out to the dimensions of a respectable farmhouse, made a mockery of the matted and tangled underbrush of the hillside it surveyed. All around us orchards and vineyards flourished, and we longed with a jealous fervor to join the legions of vintners of God's Plain.

The Faravels, our guardians and mentors, had taken us to visit Monsieur Meffre, that man of daring and vision who had from the start been pointed to as the most successful viticulturist of the valley. Monsieur Meffre had branched out from his family holdings in Gigondas to clear and till and flower the wide, flat, windswept wilderness of the whole of God's Plain between Orange and Sablet. Once an ungrateful sweep of scrub baked by summer sun and stunted by ravaging gales blowing unhindered from the north, God's Plain, under the care of Monsieur Meffre, now was carpeted in green-gold vines. Each vineyard was shielded by thick cypress trees, towering black-green ramparts against the damaging mistral wind. The great abandoned farm complexes now teemed with those Spanish families who had come to Provence to work his land.

Monsieur Meffre had branched further than God's Plain to Châteauneuf-du-Pape, that renowned mound of land where thirteen different plantings thrive, and where the emblem of the keys of Avignon is embossed on each true bottle of the pope's rich, heady wine.

One day we had been invited for *goûter*, or high tea, with the Meffres at their Second Empire château overlooking their Châteauneuf-du-Pape slopes. An extravagant place of tapestries and shining marbles, fountains and formal gardens, this massive pile of the Meffres seemed to be a folly for weekends with their children, less a home than a testament to their stone-mulched vinelands on the most blessed slopes of the

A Vineyard for La Sérafine

Rhône Valley. Charming and unpretentious people, the Meffres for the most part lived in a handsome bourgeois house backed up against their private winery in the village of Gigondas. As a man of free enterprise, Monsieur Meffre had explained that he worked apart from the system of national wine cooperatives. This fact, Monsieur Faravel told us later, made him suspect in the eyes of small vintners. We would be small vintners and in no way able to compete with the extensive Meffre holdings. Nor did we want to. Clearly our immediate associations remained not with the lofty viticulturists of Châteauneuf-du-Pape but with the more modest growers of our own village cooperative of Roaix-Séguret.

Monsieur Faravel had taken a new job at the Fabre factory in Vaison-la-Romaine, leaving him little time to work his own land. For that reason, and because of his continual, nagging back trouble, he decided to have his vineyards and orchards farmed by a neighbor, Monsieur Jean Verdeau. It was easier that way, and more fruitful. Monsieur Verdeau owned a tractor and used modern methods of spraying and pruning. Vice-president of the Roaix-Séguret wine cooperative, he was a man of unquestioned integrity and had the rare advantage of a vigorous young son who worked with him. We could have the same arrangement of *métayer,* sharing on a fifty-fifty basis with Monsieur Verdeau, and our land could produce both a superior, robust red wine and a nervous, delicious rosy wine. In addition, the Verdeau men, *père et fils,* knew all about fruit trees, and Monsieur Faravel urged us to put in an orchard like his, of plums, cherries, and apricots.

It was all we dreamed of. To flower our sun-drenched fallow soil in vines and orchards gave us an exhilarating sense of independence. Our small property of twelve acres, well-planted, could be self-sufficient, a larder of life, a refuge and a fortress for us and our families in case of the disasters of war and revolution, calamities never remote from the French mind. In more likely and happier seasons, to grow our own produce and drink our own wine would be joy unsurpassed.

Monsieur Faravel spurred us on by arranging a meeting with Monsieur Verdeau. He was our man, Monsieur Faravel assured us, and, indeed, from the minute we met Jean Verdeau, he became a staunch friend, an expert adviser, and a dour prophet.

In France, a landowner cannot just survey his acres and decide haphazardly to plant a barren hillside in vines. Viticulturists form a coveted clique. Viniculture is an art, and its artists must pursue their craft by the enlightened rules of excellence laid down for the Institut National des Appellations d'Origines and the Ministry of Agriculture in Paris. Local officials adapt the laws to their particular areas, administered in our case in Avignon, the capital of the Vaucluse.

"The wines of the Côtes-du-Rhône are strictly controled," Monsieur Verdeau warned, "and they strangle you in red tape . . . *quoi?*"

Having coped with all the details of planting and growing his own vineyards, Monsieur Verdeau took the canny approach. He knew the traps that awaited us before the first blade of the plough could be turned in the soil. The complications were valid, reaching back to the turn of the century after the French vineyards had been decimated by the *Phylloxera vastatrix*. This ravaging plant louse, brought to France from the United States, devastated the vineyards of both Europe and America. Curiously, it was the sturdy native eastern American rootstocks resistant to the grub, which the

French in turn grafted to their own *Vitis vinifera* vines, that revived the sickly grape. Since then protective legislation of the vines had grown, wth many of the first breakthroughs made by our former neighbor in Châteauneuf-du-Pape, Baron Le Roy du Boiseaumarié. Now, every minute step of wine-growing was programmed from the top.

First, the exact dimensions of our land had to be retraced. The maps of our property were in the office of the land surveyor, not in Avignon, but in Carpentras, a beautiful and lively city twenty miles south of Séguret. In Carpentras, we climbed a wide staircase and wound through the corridors of a splendid rococo building to the offices of the surveyor. To our astonishment, the brusque, burly official knew all about us as the new owners of La Sérafine, or as he called it, the Domaine des Michelons. After we produced the deed to the property, he summoned an assistant to fetch the map of our land. He ordered coffee for us from a café in the square below, and we sipped ceremoniously as the dusty pole was hung from a bookcase and the map unfurled like a banner. We couldn't believe our eyes as the official, with the aplomb of a schoolmaster, pointed a rod at every mound and rock and sinkhole of our hillside. No stone was left unturned, no cypress spire uncharted, no vine untraced.

"Voilà, the olive groves were here, a small plot of vine-yards there, orchards on these terraces, and to the east, a pleasance near the well," he informed us, adding that a wedge of pines jutting into our land belonged to someone else. Except for this unexpected foreign body, our property was shaped like a lozenge, defined by a large pine tree at the top and spreading down the hill in a wide apron to the valley.

The official surveyed not only our land but our taxes. As

orchards and olive groves were taxed far less than vinelands, he advised us to replant the terraces of fruit trees and revive our lanes of magnificent olive trees that had been blighted in the great frost of 1956. Some of the gnarled trunks had survived and were beginning to spread their silvery branches to the sun; but, as Monsieur Verdeau pointed out, it took nearly twenty years before an olive grove became productive. The picking and pressing of the olives require an extensive team of experts impossible to recruit in our region now, much less a generation hence. Apricot, cherry, and plum trees, yes, and vineyards too. Even those would take four years of back-breaking labor. Olives were a luxury . . . *quoi?*

Twenty years is a long time, the official agreed; vineyards were more to the point. In the meantime, we would be taxed —and very little—on the land as it was registered. He had no right to grant permission for the planting of vines. That would have to be arranged in Paris through the authorities in Avignon.

Before the map of our property was rolled up we examined it carefully. Paul-Marc suggested that Monsieur Verdeau arrange to have the parcel of land intruding on our prospective vineyard sold to us. The possible, but improbable, idea of someone building a weekend lodge in that knoll of pines on our eastern flank horrified us. We realized from this bird's-eye view of our domain that our farmhouse stood in the middle of our property, which was a rare thing, as most peasants' houses flank the entrance to the land, leaving the orchards and vineyards to sweep behind and beyond. We were dead center, our complex sheltered in the embrace of our amphitheater of hillside. The valley of God's Plain stretched far below. Steep mountains rose in back of us. To the east and the west we had long, sweet views of the hilltowns of Sablet and Rasteau and Roaix. If our winter world revolved around the diplomatic pace and the frenetic tensions of New York, our summer world was guarded from the eyes of others. This ancient map revealed to us the gift of silence, of space, of a private and treasured life far away in Provence. The problem was to flower our abandoned oasis.

Next, we plotted our siege of Avignon. How was the best way to assault the hive of bureaucracy that regulated the permits, first to be approved there before being sent to the hierarchy of property controllers in Paris? Like most Frenchmen, Monsieur Verdeau was convinced that he had a pipeline to the top, but better still, Paul-Marc was in contact with the chief engineer of the agricultural development of the Vaucluse. Jacques Arrighi de Casanova, a handsome and wily Corsican, was our good friend. He knew all the *grosses légumes,* the big shots who could pull strings, not only for the right to plant our vineyards, but eventually for municipal water and electricity, and better still, a telephone—all undreamed-of luxuries for our sequestered peasants' farmhouse in Séguret.

Even with this superior contact, it took weeks of driving back and forth to Avignon, countless calls on officials, and yards of paperwork before we received a bona fide go-ahead to plant two hectares of vineland. When our property was firmly established under the laws of *appellation contrôlée* of the Côtes-du-Rhône, Monsieur Verdeau and Paul-Marc selected the rootstocks for the vineyard of La Sérafine. For two and a half acres for red wine, *le rouge,* they chose the Grenache grape, high in alcoholic content, sweet in other climes, but dry and robust in our chalky surface and rocky subsoil that lock in humidity. For the two acres of *rosé* wine, they picked the Clairette rootstocks that flourish in our pebbly terrain, producing a fruity, ruby-red pink wine without a flaw of orange and of an extraordinary fourteen degrees in alcoholic content.

Everything had to be done by the book. Every step had to measure up to the standards of quality, rigidly maintained, continually subjected to the threat of the national Fraud Brigade, which descends periodically on proprietors to check their methods. Viticultural practices are sharply defined: planting, pruning, fertilizing, and the spraying of the vines. Choosing the variety of grapes was only the start of the arduous, exacting, and skillful process of growing the vine and producing the wine. Producing good wine from good vines is a pact between man and nature. Sometimes there might be a battle of wind and hail, or often an uneasy truce between abundant rainfall and excessive heat; at worst, a defeat of damaging frost and devouring parasites; at best, a triumph of tender vines blooming under benevolent skies of golden sun. Our land, we were told, had the terraced, gravelly content for a virile red and a nervous *rosé*, wines reputed more for their honesty than for their greatness.

"Eh bien, we must clear the land before we can plant," Monsieur Verdeau told Paul-Marc after they had agreed on the *métayage*, which meant we were to pay for the clearing and the vine plantings. Monsieur Verdeau and his son undertook the labor. The benefits of the first harvest went to them and from then on we split the profits down the middle.

At that, it would be a grueling conquest of the earth, without yield of grapes for three years, without a drop of wine for four. After preparing the ground, Monsieur Verdeau and Jean-Pierre had to turn the turf before planting the rootstocks

in the fertile ground, placing them far apart to allow for
space and air. During the first year, their main preoccupation
was in assuring the vines of developing solid roots. Later,
there would be the ritual of spraying, the pruning during the
time of the *débourrement,* when the leaves grow before the
fruit blossoms. In the fourth year, the grapes would be ready
to be pressed into wine, our wine from the matted tangle of
underbrush that now cluttered the slopes of La Sérafine. This
long cycle of seasons was rewarded by the great autumn festival of the harvesting of the grapes, the eternal *vendange* of
France.

For all this endless churning, tending, and culling of the
fruits of the Valley of the Rhône, there was a carrot in the
form of Agricultural Credit for the neophyte vintner. When
our soil had been analyzed by the authorities in Avignon, we
applied for a slice of credit for restoring our land. The results
of the soil analysis arrived and we came through with flying
colors. We were assured that anything would grow in our
land, which had lain fallow for fifty years. But if we had the
richest soil in the region, we would not be the richest landowners. Our request for credit was denied. No reasons given.
Just "Non" from the Crédit Agricole. A two-horned di-
lemma. Our summer holiday was drawing to a close. Decisions had to be made rapidly. Would we sacrifice the land to
the new pavilion we planned to restore, or would we give up
the gallery, the library, the comfortable dining room and
kitchen for a burgeoning vineyard? We agreed to let the new
wing ride and start tilling the soil. We were elated. Now our
property would no longer consist of a big white house standing idle most of the year on a hillside, but a pleasance of
vineyards being worked all year, a contribution to our village
of Séguret.

XI

PAGANS, POPES, AND POETS

J'ai plus des souvenirs
que si j'avais mille ans . . .

[BAUDELAIRE]

As our ties to the land and people of Séguret tightened we
became more and more curious about the history of our property in relation to our village. In clearing the slopes for our
vineyard Monsieur Verdeau had found surprising vestiges
of the past. Near the well he discovered a pair of rough granite troughs that looked old enough to be Roman, I thought,
and a heap of bleached fossils might well be the remains of
one of Caesar's legionnaires. A bit farfetched, Monsieur Verdeau decided, laughing off the bones as odd joints of a mule's

carcass, but the troughs he admitted might be ancient. While hacking away at the thornbush, he had uncovered rugged walls, stretches of dried stones with vaulted arches, obviously far older than the 1648 roof tile dating the house. Probably from the *douzième,* Monsieur Verdeau conceded, as though the twelfth century were yesterday. In a country like Provence, where the past and present walk hand in hand, people take such finds as normal, but I felt as though we had happened on our own archeological dig. I longed to know more about our domain, to delve into its history and find out what kind of people had lived there before us. We knew that peasants had built our *mas* and farmed our land, but I wondered who had inhabited our hillside centuries ago, at the time of the Romans, for instance, or of the popes of Avignon.

I suspected that our property had a special significance in the history of Séguret, not only because of its wide view of the valley, but also because it curves in a green arc between two splendid white chapels. On the summit of the mountain behind our farmhouse, we could see Notre-Dame-des-Bessons, a stark and lonely hermitage rising from a forest of spruce. Below us, in a bouquet of pines on the Girard domain, stands Saint-Jean-Baptiste-d'Orlonne, a small baroque chapel that gives its name to our region, *Le Quartier Saint-Jean.* Although both are beautiful and important landmarks of Séguret, neither church is a place of public worship. Once a year, the parish priest comes during Easter week to consecrate the private Girard chapel, but "Des-Bessons" stands neglected, too scratchy and steep a climb for the clergy, much less for communicants. For us, however, it remains a constant feast for the eyes: by day, a blanched aerie against lapis lazuli skies; at night, an eerie silhouette against the rising moon.

The chapel was so mystically placed on its peak that we had often thought it to be an outpost of the Knights Templars. How, why, who had built it there, so mystifying, inaccessible, and alone?

We had often asked but no one provided the answer until Monsieur Verdeau gave me a thin, mottled paperback entitled *Notice sur Séguret,* written by Monsieur l'Abbé A. Daniel, who had been the parish priest in 1904. It was the only history I had ever seen devoted exclusively to Séguret, a village so small that most books on Provence dismissed it in a page as a *site pittoresque classé.* I couldn't wait to get into the Abbé's book. Here, at last, were ninety-six pages filled with facts and sketches and footnotes, with one entire chapter on the churches of Séguret. I spent hours reading and translating the passages on the white chapels and on our domain, which, to my amazement, proved to have a history far richer than I had dreamed.

I discovered that our twelve acres had been part of an enormous fiefdom in the twelfth and thirteenth centuries, the property of a noble family named d'Aubusson, who had been the feudal lords of this entire mountainside. They were probably related to the d'Aubusson de Villac family of the tapestry town farther north on the river Creuse, but this branch had remained in Provence, here, on our property where their great château had dominated a complex of farmlands and a village. Arnaud d'Aubusson had been lord of the manor and the Abbé said there was some doubt as to whether he had built the first church on the summit of the fifteen-hundred-foot peak behind us, or on a lower escarpment of the hill as part of his feudal fortress. The chapel was called Notre-Dame-d'Aubusson, and I realized that the local name of "Des-Bessons" was an abbreviation.

I was delighted to find that we had been correct in assuming that the site of the chapel related to the Knights Templars. There were records of Arnaud d'Aubusson having ceded three pieces of land in his territories to the White Knights in the year 1148. One of the largest commanderies of the Templars in Provence had been located in Roaix, a hill town diagonally across the valley, and they had built a smaller seat on the foundations of a great Benedictine monastery in the fiefdom of Saint-Jean just down the road from us. This meant that the chapel of Saint-Jean rested not only on the bones of the white-robed knights but also on those of the white-robed monks. I was elated. Surely our land must have connected these two fiefdoms. I was lost in fantasies of Benedictine brothers farming our land in the seventh century and Knights of the Templars cantering up our hillside in the twelfth. I scanned the jagged rocks hoping to find a trace of the Aubusson castle, but I saw none and was desolated to read that it had been sacked and burned in 1389 by a rival lord, Roger de Beaufort, Count of Turenne.

The only consolation was the discovery of a Roman settlement among the ruins. Fragments of pottery and tiles had shown it to be called *Pagus Deobensis*. Only eighty years ago an imposing statue of the Roman god Jupiter had been dug up near here and placed in the museum of Avignon. Who knows what treasures we might come upon, I wondered, convinced now that our troughs were certainly from the days of the *Pax Romana*.

The peace of Roman France had been destroyed by hordes of barbarians from the north followed by waves of Saracens from the south. I had found other books on Provence that described the raids of the "Black Devils of the Barbary Coast" who poured across the sea in the eighth century to rape the women and pillage and burn the villages. From our vineyard we have a view of the mountains where they were finally defeated. I could imagine the swarthy Saracens with their cloaks flying and scimitars brandished as they rode their nervous mounts up these treacherous peaks of Montmirail to their death. One night, when the mistral howled outside, I read of the misery that enveloped our countryside after centuries of Moorish invasions, of how wolves roamed the valleys and the people huddled starving in their hill towns. Many Provençal writers agreed, however, that if the Saracens left a memory of cruelty and cunning, they also left a legacy of grace and music. Traces of Moorish blood showed in the lithe, dark-eyed beauty of the descendants of the women they claimed, and the Arab chants inspired the Provençal troubadours who sang in the language of Oc. One of the most famous troubadours came from Vacqueyras, a village very near to us, and the Abbé suggests that another troubadour, Jean d'Aubusson, might have been a member of the same family of noblemen that had owned our hillside.

After the defeat of the d'Aubusson family by Roger de Beaufort, our domain passed to the clergy as part of the lands of the Holy See. There were conflicting stories about the fate of the chapel of Notre-Dame-d'Aubusson. Some said it was destroyed along with the castle and replaced by a modest dwelling that served as an observation post for the collector of tithes. From this lofty vantage point, he could assess the value of the harvest of almost every farm in the community, so that no citizen of Séguret escaped paying his tenth to the Church. The papacy was all-powerful then, and rich. The wealth and lands of the Knights Templars of France had been confiscated by King Philip the Fair in 1309, the same year he had installed the first French pope, Clement V, in Avignon, a town strategically placed in Provence between the kingdom of France and the papal state of the Comtat Venaissin. Although I remembered a smattering of schoolbook history about the French popes in Avignon and the Schism of the Church, I had honestly never heard of the Comtat Venaissin until we found our place in Séguret. After a while I realized that our neighbors always referred to our region simply as *Le Comtat,* and the men called themselves *Comtadins,* and the women, *Comtadines.* We noticed at the wine festival that the boys and girls wore special costumes and danced to special music, as typical of the tradition and culture of our Countship as the midnight Mass we had seen celebrated during our first Christmas holiday at La Sérafine. Everyone in our village spoke French, and many spoke Provençal, but more than Frenchmen or Provençaux, the people guarded their identity as proud citizens of the Comtat Venaissin.

I became fascinated with our Countship because now, as owners of a farmhouse and a vineyard in Séguret, we counted as true *Comtadins.* Having traced the story of our property from the days of Caesar to the time of the Templars, I longed to know how it related to the popes. This meant collecting more books and consulting old maps that would show me the exact outline of the Comtat Venaissin. Part of the immense territory of Provence, but more precisely the heart of the present *département* of Vaucluse, the papal state reached south almost to the Lubéron Mountains and the Durance River and west to the Rhône River. It stretched east to the Countship of Sault, but the northern edge was ragged, chopped off from its enclave of Valréas that nudged the border of the *département* of Dauphiné. In addition, the Comtat was split into two parts, the upper and the lower. Séguret was one of the "perched" villages of the upper region, a peak away from the mightiest mountain of Provence, Mont Ventoux. When at last I had become oriented to the landscape and began exploring the towers and palaces and towns of our Countship, I found it as exciting as discovering a new country.

I learned that, in the immense theater of Mediterranean civilization, the Comtat Venaissin had assumed a major role in the thirteenth century. As a countship, it had been shifted back and forth among the counts of Provence, the counts of Barcelona, and the counts of Toulouse, to whom it belonged in 1209. In that fateful year, Pope Innocent III sent his crusading knights, not eastward to vanquish the infidels, but westward to the Languedoc in France to put down the Cathares, a sect of Christians considered heretics for their reformist zeal and esoteric form of worship. It was called the Albigensian Crusade, for the people, the Cathares, were known as Albigeois, and their great leader was Raymond of Toulouse. The crusade lasted for years; the slaughter was merciless. During the siege of the city of Béziers, when the crusaders asked how to distinguish between orthodox and heretic, Arnold Amaury, the Papal Legate, shouted his infamous reply: "Kill them all! God will know his own."

In 1226, a final campaign ended this graceful, brilliant, and pure civilization of the Languedoc, which was joined to the kingdom of France. The next pope, Benedict, however, decided at the Treaty of Meaux in 1229 to keep a parcel of this rich countship in Provence for himself. After decades of haggling, the Comtat Venaissin—and our village of Séguret along with it—became, in 1274, an official part of the Holy See. That was thirty-five years before the French popes had settled in Avignon. This fact debarrassed me of an idea to which I had clung obstinately: that Avignon had been the capital of the Comtat Venaissin. Stripped of its status as a republic for having sided with Raymond's heretics, Avignon was then just a windy, wall-less ruin on the Rhône. The Comtat's capital had been at Pernes-les-Fontaines, a center of chivalry and jousting matches, dominated by one of the great castles of Raymond of Toulouse.

I had seen pictures of some extraordinary frescoes there, and one day we made a pilgrimage to Pernes, now a sleepy little town about twenty miles south of Séguret. No one we asked knew where the frescoes were and we had to climb a steep, sun-baked lane to the Town Hall to find the keeper of the keys. He led us back to the Tower of Ferrande and up a narrow flight of steps to a small square room at the top. Suddenly, a sequence of scratched and weathered marvels unfurled before our eyes. On one wall, a great-eyed monolithic madonna held the Christ Child on her lap. On another wall, a fierce black Saracen on a red horse battled with a white knight. The most significant panel of all, however, portrayed Pope Clement IV presenting the Bull of Investiture for the Kingdom of Naples to Charles of Anjou. We were enchanted by this rare document of the times. It appeared that the Pope, his mitre slightly askew, seemed almost to be teasing Charles, who knelt at his feet, his long hair crowned in gold, his almond eyes on the coveted bull that would extend his kingdom from Provence to Naples. Charles was the younger brother of Saint Louis, King Louis IX of France, who had taken over the Languedoc from Raymond of Toulouse. Through a slit window, the guide showed us the graceful grille work of Raymond's bell tower, all that was left of his great castle that had housed the Pope's Legate until 1320, when Carpentras succeeded Pernes-les-Fontaines as the capital of the Comtat Venaissin.

Unlike Pernes that hid its secrets from us in a tall, dark tower, Carpentras seemed an open book, its centuries of history mirrored in the faces of its people. All we had to do was walk through the winding cobbled streets and brush up against the figures in this landscape to realize that Carpentras had always been a crossroads of Mediterranean civilization. Especially the young girls showed strains of their Italian and Spanish bloodlines, and many of the boys had the quick intelligent look of the Sephardics who had taken refuge here at the time of the popes, building the oldest synagogue in France and translating the classics of Hebrew and Arabic.

Since we have been in Séguret, we have come to know many other faces of Carpentras. The traits of style, elegance, and humanity with which the city cares for its aged and infirm in the baroque Hôtel-Dieu, given to Carpentras two hundred years ago by its greatest benefactor, Bishop Malachie d'Inguimbert. We have understood, too, the muscular profile of commerce of Carpentras, twenty miles to the south of our village and a flourishing center of trade. Now that the orchards of La Sérafine are producing, we often accompany Monsieur Verdeau to the huge farmer's market to sell our kilos of apricots, cherries, and plums. Hundreds of growers come from miles around. We all gather at dawn in the huge esplanade to pile our mounds of produce in front of our trucks as the buyers saunter up and down, judging the goods and bargaining for low prices. Not a word is spoken. Offers are passed back and forth on slips of paper until a nod on both sides fixes the deal. Usually the grower comes out on the short end, we discovered, having not only to grow, pick, and cull the produce, but also to transport it to the shipper. After hauling our heavy boxes onto the scales, we watched the dispatcher fix a fancy plastic wrapper over our fruits of Séguret and send them off to be sold as produce of Carpentras at three times his price in markets all over Europe. In addition to being a place to sell, Carpentras is also a place where we go to buy, often shopping at the *Prisunic,* a five-and-ten and supermarket in front of the Palace of Justice. One day, while having a drink at the next-door café, we saw an ordinary scene that, to me, seemed to embody the spirit and harmony of this city and its citizens.

The great bells of the Cathedral of Saint-Siffrein began to thunder across the square and we looked up to see a funeral procession emerging from the church. There was nothing very unusual about a burial except that in one short moment the entire range of the great periods of history of the city were suddenly brought into focus. I realized that the funeral Mass had been celebrated at a baroque altar near a chapel holding the relics of Saint Mors, not a human, but the bit of Constantine's horse formed from two nails of the True Cross, and the sixth-century relics of Siffrein, patron saint of Carpentras. From the flamboyant Gothic cathedral—built by order of the antipope Benedict XIII, at the time of the Great Schism—the coffin had been carried through the Jewish Gate carved on a Renaissance façade to the boom of bells from Romanesque spires. Then the mourners had driven by a Roman arch on a seventeenth-century square past a twentieth-century supermarket to a medieval graveyard. There in a flash is Carpentras, I thought, its great riches as much a tribute to the dead as a joy for the living. Although on the surface it may appear a typical provincial town of France, at heart Carpentras retains the same aplomb and dignity that marked its splendor as the capital of the Comtat Venaissin for five hundred years.

If Carpentras impressed us as a city of many faces, Avignon seemed a city of many moods, brimming with life, high-spirited and young, and at the same time intensely aware of its papal heritage. As the fast trains from Paris stop there, we are always driving twenty miles down the valley to meet friends coming to see us *en* Avignon, because you go to Avignon as you would go to a country, rather than to a city, such as *à* Madrid. Although now merely the capital of our *département*, the Vaucluse, Avignon retains its thirteenth-century status as a republic. A hundred years later it became the most powerful and magnificent citadel of Europe when seven French popes ruled all of Christendom from the Rock of the Lord. Now, some of these resonances of grandeur come alive in the floodlit Papal Palace where we often see theater productions in the cobbled Court of Honor. Peering up at the lighted windows I try to imagine Pope Clement VI in the Hall of Justice. His tower, which he decorated with an enchantment of impious frescoes of nymphs and hunters in pastoral pleasures, is one of the few interior spaces that evokes the former pomp and elegance of this massive pile.

Clement was the fourth and most kingly pope to reign in Avignon, and I found him to be the most fascinating of the pontiffs. It was he who bought Avignon for the Holy See, making it a papal state by the Comtat Venaissin. That was in 1348, a key year in the history of our Countship. The year when the beautiful young Queen Joanna I of Naples and Provence traveled from Italy to Avignon to obtain the papal blessing absolving her of all guilt in the brutal assassination of her first husband and permitting her to marry her cousin. In return, Joan gave Avignon to Clement for a paltry eighty thousand florins. For five hundred years thereafter, the city with its glorious palaces encircled by miles of crenelated walls and dominated by the towering Rock of the Lord above the bridge where *on y danse tous en rond* remained one of the richest jewels in the papal cloak. The people of Avignon claim that their *rondes* were never danced on the skinny, sturdy bridge built by Saint Bénézet in 1185, but under its arches on the green meadows of the Island of Barthelasse. When we are in Avignon and the streets burn with heat, we escape to lunch on this island. From under the plane trees we marvel at the steep white towers of the popes and the graceful spans of Bénézet's bridge jutting halfway across the rapid, swirling currents of the river Rhône.

In reading of the joyous festivals that Pope Clement had celebrated on this island, I came upon a description of a fleeting encounter here between Laura and Petrarch. It sent me scurrying for the sonnets, for in my ignorance, I had always thought of Petrarch as purely an Italian poet. I had pictured his famous lines of *chiare, fresche e dolci acque* as an evocation of the clear, fresh, and sweet waters of Tuscany rather than those of the rushing river at Fontaine-de-Vaucluse, a calm, leafy village in our Countship ten miles south of Avignon. Laura, the beloved of Petrarch, had been as nebulous to me as Beatrice, the beloved of Dante, and in my imagination, as Florentine. It came as a revelation to learn that Laura was an Avignonnaise and that Petrarch had spent most of his life in and around the Papal Court of Avignon.

True, he had been born in Tuscany, but at the age of ten

had been brought by his parents to Carpentras, where he passed his youth before attending the universities of Bologna and Montpellier. At twenty, Francesco Petrarch went to Avignon to garner favor at the Papal Court, where in time he became the most famous chronicler, cleric, poet, and scholar of the century. He traveled widely but always returned to the Vaucluse. It was not only the popes that held him in Avignon—for he despised the extravagance and corruption of the court—but also Laura.

Petrarch was twenty-three when he first laid eyes on Laura in the Church of Saint-Clare on the morning of April 6, 1327. From that moment, and even after her death of the black plague twenty-one years later, Petrarch was held captive of an unrequited love. Two of the most noble and celebrated lovers of history, they hardly spoke. Petrarch never divulges the full name of Laura nor the exact color of her eyes. It was enough for him to gaze from afar upon her massed gold hair and her angelic mouth filled with pearls and roses to be drawn into a passion that, for a lifetime, he celebrated in five thousand lines of lover's plaints and praises. It struck me as odd that Laura should have been so cold to Petrarch, who is described as tall, handsome, with olive skin, dark hair, and brilliant eyes betraying all the fire of his genius. Some say that Laura never existed, except as an inspiration for the sonnets. Others claim that she was the wife of Hugues de Sade and the mother of eleven children, an image hardly fitting that of the nymph or goddess coming up from the clearest depths of the river Sorgue envisioned by the poet. Certainly Laura lived in the heart of Petrarch, for he never escaped the bondage of love, even after he had sired two natural children, even after he had fled to seclusion in Fontaine-de-Vaucluse. Off and on for sixteen years Petrarch lived a quasi-hermit's life there, writing his books and sonnets, cultivating his garden, roaming the banks of the river whose "waters tell of love, and so do the branches and the airs, the birds, the fish, the grasses and the blossoms— they all cry together love, love forever . . ."

The fountain now is too known, this Closed Valley of the Romans, which gives its name, Vaucluse, to our *département* of France. Busloads of visitors crowd the cafés that emblazon their awnings with lovers' names. The best hours I have spent following in the footsteps of Petrarch have been in the early morning, climbing through the wooded lane to the deep mysterious cavern that disgorges a powerful rush of water over the rocks to the river Sorgue below. The little house that the guide showed me as belonging to Petrarch seems too dreary and dark a place to have contained the spirit of the wordly cleric and poet laureate of Rome. I had read he had lived further up the hill near the Fountain, dressing like a peasant, eating figs, nuts, and river fish, with only his dog, his faithful servant, and his books for company. "All the works that have come out of my pen," he wrote, "were either entirely composed, begun, or conceived at Vaucluse." His copy of the *Confessions of St. Augustine* was his constant companion, the book that he read at the summit of Mont Ventoux.

Francesco Petrarch and his brother, Gherardo, were probably among the first mountaineers to scale the isolated massive dome that dominates our county of Venaissin. "I was stupefied by the vivacity of the air, the immensity of space," Petrarch wrote of that ascent in 1336, and I felt much the same way the day that our entrepreneur, Robert Charrasse, had driven us to the summit, taking the corkscrew turns with the chilling skill of a race driver. To me, this curiously bald and windy mountain with its enormous view to the Alps is both stupefying and frightening. Perhaps I am not yet deeply enough imbued with the mystique of Provence, for to the Provençaux this haughty wind-swept hump is both Mount Olympus and Mount Hymettus in one. Not only Petrarch, but all the great Provençal poets have sung its praises, especially the *Félibriges,* the group of writers of the nineteenth century that revived the customs and lore of Provence under the guidance of Frédéric Mistral. Mistral, who provoked a renascence of the Provençal language, also assaulted Ventoux to plant the gonfalon of the *Félibriges* on the summit. His name, the same as our wind, Mistral, is the Provençal word for master. It is this master wind, along with the sun, the water, and the mountains, that contributes so much to the personality of our Countship and to our village of Séguret.

Once I had established the identity of our Countship I came back to the history of our village. Séguret, or the Latin Seguretum, comes from the word *segur,* according to the parish priest, the Abbé A. Daniel, a place where one is safe. Our village, clasped around a mountain high above the plain, offered its citizens protection behind high walls that reached from the fortress on the hilltop to the cluster of houses far below. Not that Séguret was completely impervious to attack. We had noticed an engraved plaque mounted in the square of the Church of Saint-Denis that gives a thumbnail, and somewhat gory, sketch of the vicissitudes that beset our village. Its dates go back to the time of the invasions of the Greeks and Romans to the most recent tragedy on June 10, 1944, when five patriots of Séguret had been executed by the Nazi invaders.

Pestilence and epidemics had taken their toll as well as wars. An outbreak of smallpox in 1871 reduced the number of villagers from fourteen hundred to nine hundred at the turn of the century. Vintners abandoned their vineyards when the pitiless phylloxera plant louse decimated their vines. But the olive groves and orchards bloomed, and in 1904 the Abbé notes that Séguret flaunted an establishment of silkworm cocoons for sericulture. I was interested to read that a new commerce had sprung up with the importation of American vine plantings to revive the ailing vineyards. At that time there were two oil presses, a hospital run by nuns, three cafés, two butchers, three grocers, and a half dozen government employees. Although one hundred and thirty citizens, all men, voted, municipal services were scarce, Séguret having neither a postman nor a *diligence* for public transport.

Monsieur l'Abbé A. Daniel would turn over in his ivy-clad grave if he knew that his beloved village now counts only seven hundred and twenty-five citizens, of which the majority of voters—including women—vote the Socialist or Communist ballot, as these parties in France protect the small landowner. There is no longer a factory of any kind, only one grocer, one Sunday café run by an Andorran, church attendance is minimal, but Séguret supports two postmen, a lively discothèque, a September wine festival, and a traditional midnight Mass, *Die Bergers de Séguret,* that is performed every Christmas in his own beautiful Church of Saint-Denis.

I was not surprised to read in the Abbé's history that the Principality of Orange had been the enduring enemy of Séguret. To me, Orange seemed solemn and wind-lashed, somehow lacking the warmth and luster of other cities around us, perhaps because it had never been part of our Countship, but a Huguenot island within the papal state. At one time, in the sixteenth century, it had belonged to Holland and the Royal House of Nassau had added the name of Orange to its title. The princes had ripped the marbles off the Roman theater and Caesar's arch for their palaces, and fortified castles along their special highway, the Route of the Princes of Orange, that wound down the Plain of God beneath Séguret and further, to Buis-les-Baronnies and Nyons. Not only a Protestant stronghold during the Wars of Religion, Orange had been autonomous for centuries under a series of Williams of Orange, ever since 973 when William the Liberator had driven the Moors from the city. Even before, during the *Pax Romana*, when the town nearest us, Vaison-la-Romaine, had been a peaceful hub of trade, Orange had stood apart, serving as an important military garrison. Then, the great Augustan theater had been built for cruel bread-and-circus spectacles for the thousands of legionnaires stationed there.

Thousands of people still come to see plays and ballets in the immense amphitheater of Orange and at night from our terrace we can see the floodlights glowing ten miles away. I suppose that the villagers of Séguret could always have seen the lights of Orange from their mountain perch, and must have looked at them with dread, especially when the Calvinists came after the Catholics. Twice in fifteen years they had laid siege to Séguret. The first time, on May 25, 1563, the village was taken by surprise in the middle of the night when the forces, under the command of Lieutenant Funeau de St.-Auban, scaled the walls and massacred one hundred and thirty citizens of Séguret. I could imagine the terror and bloodshed, for the streets were as narrow and twisting then as they are now, and the victims had no means of escape. I was glad to read that the second attack proved a victory for our village, and the Abbé gives the event the suspense of a thriller.

It seems that the wary commander of Séguret became suspicious of a young man named Blaise Bermond and had him arrested. Indeed, a battle plan of Séguret had been found in his pocket, and he confessed to having given the defense secrets of his village as payment for his gambling debts to the commander of Orange. To obtain pardon, however, Bermond turned counteragent, offering to trap the Huguenots of Orange inside the ramparts of Séguret. Four hundred horsemen and foot soldiers advanced on our village, mounted their ladders, and began climbing the walls. Just as they were about to leap into the fire of the waiting defenders, two nervous soldiers triggered their guns, warning the attackers, who fled down the valley. This victory cost Séguret only two men. They were buried, like the victims before them, under the nave of the Church of Saint-Denis. In those days, people were buried standing up, cheek to jowl. Our friend Monsieur André Charrasse, whose ancestors had fought in these battles of Séguret, told us of a hair-raising experience when he had once worked as a master mason on the restoration of the church. In the course of repairing the floor, one of the workmen had dug up a deeply embedded stone under the nave. From the yawning hole a ghastly stench emerged, followed by a sudden and terrifying noise, strangely like a rattle of bones disjointing and collapsing into a heap. Monsieur Charrasse was convinced that air had penetrated the mass grave and he had heard disintegrating the skeletons of the heroes that had fallen in battle three hundred and fifty years before.

Every time I go to the Church of Saint-Denis, I think of the heroes beneath the stones, not with a shudder, but with a certain pride in the gallant heritage of our village, which had contributed its share to the glory of our Countship. That papal glory lasted until the French Revolution when, in 1791, the Comtat Venaissin and the State of Avignon joined with France. It was not such an easy break, however, as the actual treaty was not signed until 1797, and finally ratified as late as 1814.

During this period, the hillside where our property lies had been sliced up and sold in big lots to private landholders. A new chapel of Saint-Jean-Baptiste-d'Orlonne had been built on the foundations of the old Benedictine and Templars monasteries. From all I could gather, the tower of the tithe collector at the summit of our mountain of d'Aubusson had long since disappeared in favor of the white hermitage that we see every day when we are at La Sérafine.

When the Abbé explored the present chapel, he found the date 1771 carved on the vaulted portal. Even at that time, in the eighteenth century, he believed that Notre-Dame-d'Aubusson could never have been a parish church because of its position on such a remote pinnacle. He asked the people of Séguret about this mysterious chapel, but no one seemed to know exactly who had built it there or why. Some people told a strange legend of the mountaintop having been haunted. For years, agonizing cries and weird chants echoed through the woodland until the terrified inhabitants decided to band together and erect this chapel to insure their protection by the Queen of Heaven. Once the church was built, miraculously the evil spirits vanished. Others told a different, and far more romantic, story of a young noblewoman who, when expecting her first child, prayed to the Virgin for a safe delivery. After being delivered of beautiful twins, she and her husband rendered homage to the Virgin Mary by building this chapel in her honor.

At the time of the Abbé, little girls, after their first Communion, scaled this highest and steepest peak of Séguret to lay their wreaths at the feet of the statue of the Virgin. Now, the white hermitage remains deserted, and although we count it as a special blessing, so far we have never had the courage to assault the sheer rockface guarding Notre-Dame-d'Aubusson.

Our postman, Monsieur Georges Giely, keeps urging us to climb up by a shorter way behind the fortress above our village. His ancestors had lived in Séguret for centuries, and the Abbé mentions members of the Giely family as having been administrators of the town in the eighteenth century. He also speaks of the prominent forebears of our friends the Charrasse family, and of the Aymards, relatives of our carpenter, and of the Meffre family, to whom our domain had belonged since the early nineteenth century.

"La montagne Meffre," the vast hillside had been called, Monsieur Régis Meffre told us when he came to see us, unable to believe his eyes at the transformation of the old farmhouse. Although the place had belonged to his family, they had never lived there. The peasant who had tended the olives and the vines was a farmer, an employee of theirs. After he died the property had been abandoned, remaining so through the Leschi's tenure, until we brought it back to life.

We had liked the name Madame Leschi had given the farmhouse, La Sérafine, so much so that we had decided to keep it. To me, the seraphim above the Plain of God seemed particularly apt. To this day, however, the people of Séguret still call our place Le Domaine des Michelons, or simply, Les Michelons. It has no special meaning in Provençal, our friends tell us, and they have no idea of its origin. The only person who has ever come up with a clue was Monsieur Giely, who suggested that perhaps someone named Michel had lived there long ago and christened his property Michelons. "Voilà, Michel . . . Michelons," he decided on the spot and it seemed a perfectly reasonable answer.

MAÎTRESSE DE
MAISON

Je vis de bonne soupe
et non de beau langage . . .

[MOLIÈRE, *Les Femmes Savantes*]

September, when we had last gone to Provence, had been too late in the season for the family to come, except for Beau-Père, a widower and retired, who had the leisure of his whims. Now, the lofty new wing was finished, if not completely furnished, and I wrote to my sister in Spain asking her to come for a few weeks in July with her husband, an American Air Force general, and their three children. Paul-Marc launched invitations with extravagant largesse, and his children, Jacques and Nicole, promised to spend as much time with us as they could spare from the Côte d'Azur. Jacques and Beau-Père were already installed in La Sérafine, and Paul-Marc announced happily that everyone would be coming as we drove from the Marseilles airport to our village in the Vaucluse. On his way back and forth to spring conferences in Europe, he had detoured to Provence for an inspection of construction and I longed to see our new kitchen, the dining room off the terrace, and the battered old stable, now a high-ceilinged library with a fieldstone fireplace and wooden gallery.

"The house is perfect now, you will see," Paul-Marc exclaimed, swinging the car up our smoothed and coiling road banked in yellow broom and into the weedy esplanade in front of the new west wing. Bête-Noire, our black poodle, sprang from the window and to the front door and I followed, somewhat slowed down by the long night flight from New York.

Inside, an assortment of white-metal garden chairs were ranged around the Louis Quinze desk; the end leaves had been pulled out to make a dining table and straw mats placed around.

Two delicious creatures in bikinis rattled knives and forks, moving voluptuously over the red tiles as they laid the table. Jacqui lifted himself languidly from a mat on the terrace and appeared at the window, calling a cool greeting and introducing Anne and Catherine, one a deeply tanned blonde, one a pale brunette, who came over to shake hands limply.

Beau-Père rushed in, kissing us on both cheeks. "Bon, at last you are here, just in time for lunch! Mes enfants, twelve thirty, à table, à table." He pulled out a chair, cracked off an end of bread, and poured himself a glass of wine.

"Sit down, don't do anything. You can unpack later. First we will have something to eat." Paul-Marc steered me to a chair and I stripped off my jacket, feeling sticky and sleepy. As the girls slipped in from the kitchen with a *salade niçoise,* I had a chance to look around at the new dining room. Sun flowed in from the small-paned windows onto bone-white walls and plastered ceilings. A big black spider had settled in one high corner weaving a luminous web. Crumbs sprinkled the red-tiled floor and Monsieur Bonell's wiring stood out in sharp relief against the woodwork. "You are forbidden to go into the kitchen . . . the girls will do everything today," Jacqui insisted as Anne and Catherine brought in a platter of lamb chops.

"But I want to see my new kitchen, please let me," I protested. "It must be the most modern kitchen Provence has ever known."

"It will be, it will be. Monsieur Aymard has not quite finished his cabinets," Beau-Père warned as I crossed the threshold.

So this was my dreamy Americanized kitchen that the handsome, red-haired carpenter had taken six months to plan! The polished brown cabinets were half assembled, one Formica shelf left a gaping hole below. The wretched little stove stood far shy of the cupboards, and the refrigerator was placed alone against another wall.

Everyone was happily dumping soiled dishes in a heap, oblivous to the mess. "Monsieur Aymard has promised to come and finish it tomorrow," said Jacques as I showed my dismay.

From the pandemonium of the kitchen we moved to the new library, where a beautiful and massive chimney of fieldstone covered one wall and a steep wooden staircase led to the gallery above. Powdery ashes from last night's fire crusted the hearth and billowed like sagebrush over the black marble floor. Dirt crunched underfoot as we trailed through the bar and the living room. Upstairs in our room wasps danced off the beams and clouds of hazy dust wafted through the sun-rays from the open window. An orange-varnished wall cut the hayloft room in half, and a hideous door of rough glass swung from bright brass hinges opening to an enormous new bathroom. Inside a high French bathtub three feet by seven crowded a wash basin, a w.c., and a bidet. Swags of cobwebs hung in every corner and furry brown earwigs climbed the white walls.

"Why don't you relax and have a siesta?" Paul-Marc suggested benignly, completely impervious to the grime.

"Relax? Have a siesta?" I muttered. "I couldn't close my eyes until this place is cleaned!"

"Darling, don't be hysterical. You will alienate everyone here who has worked so hard to finish the house for us."

"Alienate them? They are alienating me. We must get Monsieur Bonell to remove this ghastly swimming pool of a tub. And Monsieur Aymard to push back this insane wall and finish his cabinets in the kitchen."

I flew downstairs and found Jacqui relaxed as a lizard in the sun. "Please take the car and the girls and go and find all the brooms and soap powder and dust cloths you can. Your rooms must be pigsties."

"Just a few scorpions here and there, tant pis, we're in the country . . . but if you insist . . ."

I cleaned all afternoon, dusting, scrubbing, shaking blankets out of windows, swabbing tiles, brooming cobwebs off ceilings. Jacqui and the girls fled to a café in town and Paul-Marc and Beau-Père vanished in panic to alert the recalcitrant carpenter. By the time they returned, furniture had been replaced, the house had a sheen of glory, and I was in a state of collapse. I barely had time for a trickly shower in Monsieur Bonell's mammoth tub before Nicole arrived with her cousin.

For dinner, we set tables on the terrace and watched the moon rise like an enormous silver halo over the hermitage on the hill. Beau-Père and Paul-Marc were as delighted as Jacqui with the girls in skin-tight pants buckled under their tanned navels. When Jacqui brought out his records everybody began to dance. It was a gala housewarming for everyone but me. I slipped away, groggy with exhaustion, my American dreams of perfection shattered by the lamentable squalor of my house.

The next morning the sun smiled and so did I, propped up having breakfast in bed. Beau-Père's wobbly rendition of Massenet's "Élégie" sang through the courtyard. Footsteps crunched over the gravel. "Bonjour, beauté," Paul-Marc called down to Nicole from our window.

"Thanks for bringing the croissants and coffee in bed. You make me feel more the pampered maîtresse than the badgered maîtresse de maison."

"One doesn't exclude the other," Paul-Marc replied, kissing me. "That's life, French life, anyway. Come on, we must go to market. The Fabres are coming for lunch!"

From that day onward, a procession of friends came and went. No sooner had Jacques and Nicole left for the Côte d'Azur than a Sudanese diplomat arrived. As his red Peugeot sped down the hill a white Citroën sped up with friends from New York. Dons came from Oxford, UNESCO people from Paris, and FAO colleagues from Rome. Séguret was far from the unfindable village I feared it would be.

No matter how many people came and went or what their culinary wishes, Beau-Père clung to his own gastronomy. Springy, as wispy as a plume, his physical architecture completely belied his capacity as a consumer. Up with the birds, he split his two *petit déjeuners* of *café au lait* and croissants with an hour or two of practicing his fiddle. After a three-mile jaunt to post his pithy correspondence at the PTT of Séguret, he settled down for a *casse-croûte* of onion soup or tripes with a beaker of wine before joining us for the drive to market in Vaison. At midday, Beau-Père, ravenous again, liked to spend hours at table over a hot dinner with two wines and cheeses, followed by strong black coffee and *un petit digestif,* usually a snifter of cognac. For *goûter* at five, a jug of wine, a chunk of bread, and a slab of pâté sustained him until supper, which began preferably with a bowl of soup sturdy enough to stand a spoon in. The care and feeding of Beau-Père became an uproarious drama at La Sérafine, everyone wondering in astonishment how he kept so slim. "Les bons coqs sont maigres . . ."—good cocks are thin—he would laugh, his mischievous eyes lighting on our assemblage of international friends, all of whom fell under his spell. Beau-Père was delighted. In his heart of hearts, he loathed the country, missing the cafés and the excitement of city life. But he began to accept La Sérafine now with so many people to chat with, the palms of so many pretty women to read, such a captive audience for his afternoon concerts!

The visit of my American family, the Donovans, created another challenge, a three-cornered linguistic sparring in French, English, and Spanish. My sister, Peggy, spoke French, but her husband, Stanley, as a military officer posted in Spain, was more fluent in Spanish. Of the children, Diana, at thirteen, had studied enough French to get along, but Sheila, eleven, and Eric, nine, clung to Castilian or English. This was fodder to Beau-Père, who instantly started classes in French alternating with lessons on the violin.

Although La Sérafine was hardly a paragon as yet, the days passed blissfully with all of us *en famille* and we loved having our American family in our Provençal farmhouse. Every morning Sheila rushed to the window, flinging open the shutters to announce "another shiny day." The sun shone hotter and hotter, glazing the hillside in diamond heat. Not a drop of rain fell and the well diminished to a trickle. At noon we closed the shutters and stayed in the cool, thick-walled house. When the evening breeze rose, we sprawled on the terrace, the children shooting their rifles at Monsieur Verdeau's infant fruit trees in the orchard below.

"You'll kill the plums," Monsieur Verdeau cautioned one day as a pellet grazed his shoulder. From then on, they took turns aiming at the tins of *tripe à la mode de Caen* we had eaten for lunch. "The children won't touch all this garlicky rich food," my sister had warned, but the hamburgers and ketchup went begging as they devoured the *pistou* and *aïoli* and artichokes of Provence.

Régine Fabre invited us all to Chanteduc for dinner in her garden. The Fabres still lived in the Vaison town house, but Régine had finished her Provençal *mas* sufficiently to open it to close friends. Her three boys were the same age as the Donovan children and lack of a common language in no way barred their friendship. It was an unforgettable night, the stars dimming as a full moon rose over Mont Ventoux, washing the terrace in gold. Roger was a disarming host, and Régine entranced my tall, good-looking brother-in-law from Maine as she directed her dinner party.

Everything had been transported up the hill: the food, the silver, and the glazed Provençal pottery all laid on the ping-pong table covered in an ocher antique paisley shawl. After the hors d'oeuvres, huge platters of *couscous* were brought on. What a triumph! Only Régine could have thought of it. We all exclaimed in admiration. Before leaving she showed us the interior of Chanteduc. The same primitive little rooms in which we had stayed a few years before were now exquisite. Chanteduc was a Provençal doll's house, almost too perfect to believe. It had taken Régine almost three years to realize her ideal and, as yet, not one member of the family had spent a night in the house.

"Next summer it will be exactly as I want it," she explained. "Then we will spend our holidays here at Chanteduc."

Her strength of character amazed and humbled me. To think we had suffered through all the growing pains of La Sérafine, shivering through a Christmas holiday, sizzling through summers, inviting friends to a half-furnished shell, alternately loving and loathing every minute of it, but driven by the power of possession and the distortion of dreams to live with our farmhouse as it evolved from a heap of stones to a hearth. Compared to the Eden of Chanteduc, La Sérafine seemed a basket of snakes. Without a doubt, Régine Fabre exemplified the perfect French *maîtresse de maison*.

According to Beau-Père, consummate femininity consisted of a creature half-toy, half-slave, created for man, alternately to serve and entertain: to slough off drudgery with unflagging and unmentioned devotion, to grace the table with ineffable elegance, to keep conversation at a discreet and witty bubble, to wear womanly charm like a loose shift of chain mail, allowing, of course, for a few seductive chinks in the armor.

As a *maîtresse de maison* in Provence I had to admit that my armor was riddled with chinks, far more vulnerable than seductive, revealing unbending American rebellion in the baffling conquest of French *douceur de vivre*. Although armed with a battery of cookbooks, everything from the copious French *La Cuisine de Tante Marie* to the American culinary bible, *Mastering the Art of French Cooking*, my kitchen skirmishes invariably ended in a strategic retreat if not total defeat. "Ah, ma pauvre petite, you Americans don't *understand* food. We French are connoisseurs," Beau-Père invariably decried as he delved into one of my hissing casseroles, upbraiding me for having omitted some essential ingredient, such as the calves' foot in a *pot-au-feu*.

We fought our private war on the battleground of the kitchen tiles. Furtively, I plotted my personal revolution to overthrow the rigid French regime, bogged down in outmoded methods, enslaving the *maîtresse de maison* in the shackles of mess sergeant to an invasion of ravenous troops. Imperceptibly, I would sneak in changes, converting the French to the obvious delights of American efficiency.

On every trip I brought over American things for my Provençal house: soft percale sheets, fitted and flowered, so much cooler than the heavy linen French ones that drape over bolsters and engulf you like a winding sheet; velvety towels and mats and matching shower curtains to brighten the bathrooms. My amusing gadgets, such as an electric knife and blender and can opener and toaster, no one used, preferring the Provençal *batterie de cuisine*. Packets of plastic liners for the garbage pails proved to be essential, as Séguret had no sanitation department and the villagers had no intention of ever paying taxes for one, being quite content to heave the rubbish over the cliffside. Whatever housewares I could slip into my forty-four pounds of baggage was never enough. I sometimes wished an enormous American department store would appear like a mirage in the square of Vaison-la-Romaine and disappear the following day, giving me just enough time to stock up on all the wonderfully work-saving devices so difficult to find in provincial France. But esthetics, I discovered, far outweighed function.

In the long run my tactics proved an uphill struggle ending in a workable truce. I wanted all the gleaming American appliances, a freezer, a dishwasher, and a dispose-all to compensate for the legendary village girl who never appeared. To me, living in the country meant all-hands-on-deck in the kitchen for preparing a hearty dinner, and for lunch, a rustic picnic of a hunk of cheese, a loaf of bread, and a jug of wine under the linden tree. But Beau-Père was a hard-rock traditionalist. The good table is a way of life, especially in the provinces of France, where time is not of the essence. A fine big dining-room table was far more to the point than a dishwasher, he insisted, and all the French family agreed, overriding my desire for anything functional.

Humbly, I had to submit but with the condition that we please select the new table together. I had seen too many glasses of wine toppled over, too many husky elbows planted, and too many fists come banging down on our antique table to want anything but the sturdiest board in the dining room.

Monsieur Laffanour, in the town of Jonquières, made exactly what we wanted. A thick walnut slab on rounded fat legs, girded with tough stretchers, and long enough to seat ten comfortably. We ordered two armchairs and eight tall ladder-back chairs with rush seats to go with the table. Beau-Père and Paul-Marc were in heaven. Now they had a proper dining room in which to serve their Pantegruelian midday meals.

Satisfied with their victory they compromised by letting me inject a certain American order into our suppers on the terrace.

In the cool of the evening I was allowed an elaborate kind of picnic, making omelettes or Southern fried chicken at the table in an electric skillet I had brought from New York. Usually, we started with a platter of pungent, ruby-red Provençal tomatoes, the sweetest in the world, sprinked with fresh taragon and onions, then a bowl of country soup, before the main course, ending with green salad, cheeses, and fruits. There were always carafes of wine and long loaves of fresh bread. A miserably spare and unimaginative spread in the opinion of the French master chefs, but bait for my relinquishing all claims and refraining from any carping censorship of their takeover of the kitchen at noon.

At lunch the system, or lack of it, was strictly Gallic. Paul-Marc had blossomed into a *maître queux* in New York, preferring his own delectable dishes to those of restaurants. Beau-Père knew exactly how every dish should be prepared and served as assistant, an expert *marmiton*. He fixed the things he wanted. Fresh cucumbers, left to drain in *gros sel*, crystal salt, never the *sel fin* (fine salt would never *fatiguer* cucumbers to his liking). Together they spent hours slopping about the kitchen, concocting all sorts of delicacies from eels or fishes to roasts to casseroles. Swarms of ants and the buzzing of flies bothered them not at all. Every pot, pan, and mixing bowl was at the ready. Every counter space a clutter of peelings; every seasoning sprinkled helter-skelter. "One glass for the pot, one for the chefs," they exclaimed joyously, fortifying themselves with liters of inspiring Côtes-du-Rhône *rouge* and *rosé*. They were madly jealous of their art, allowing intruders only to whiff the tantalizing aromas drifting from the fire, or to undertake the more menial tasks of dressing the table, cutting the bread, or swinging the basket of salad. No matter what the weather, even if the temperature soared to a hundred degrees in the shade, they insisted on a steamy four-course lunch with all of us nailed to the groaning board like Strasbourg geese. Every one of their meals was a ceremony, a festival of conversation, an homage to the great civilization of France.

Any shortcuts or simplifications that I suggested were met by arch reminders from Beau-Père that France had taken centuries to develop the great art of cookery and needed no upstart improvisations from a country reputed to mangle, adulterate, and emasculate food. Everything must be fresh, few canned goods, and no frozen packages . . . *quelle horreur!* The trouble was that we spent every waking moment either preparing the meals, eating them, washing up after them, or shopping for them. It was a mania. Our days became so fanatic and viscerally oriented that I ached to forget the cuisine for a while. Often, we would start out for a day of touring, but at twelve thirty sharp, Beau-Père's stomach went off like an alarm clock. Out came the Michelin guide and, after examining the forks and spoons and stars, we would race to the nearest and best restaurant, settling in happily for a long afternoon's lunch. No amount of pressure changed the pace. Beau-Père, a master of the "*Système D*"—the *débrouillard*—the admired, wangling craft of the winner, invariably got his way, and the more he devoured the more wraithlike he became. Food was his muse, music his mistress.

The supply for this *abondance* of liquids and solids became another ritual, the marketing, the French constant *de faire les courses*. On Tuesday mornings the great outdoor market came to our neighboring town, Vaison-la-Romaine. Caravans of vendors drove in their trucks during the night and unloaded their stalls of produce in the Place de Montfort and four long, leafy avenues of the town. There were racks of flowered dresses, tables of plastic basins and pitchers, pots and pans swinging from hooks, nails and hardware and *boule* sets, ropes and chains and harnesses, and nylon underwear waving in the great square. On the Square of the Eleventh of November, dealers sold tires, pottery, and glassware, and peasants weighed enormous sacks of lime blossoms used for infusions and baths to calm the nerves.

A briny smell of seaweed emanated from the wooden planks of fishmongers, burly Marseillais in rubber boots hacking steaks of fresh tuna, offering a mussel, crying the freshness of their sole and mullet and squirming crayfish. Further on, the *charcutiers* sold pork sausages, blood sausages, Alsatian hams, and innards. Round heads of garlic woven in braided ribbons swung from one stall next to enormous baskets of black olives. Every kind of vegetable imaginable, artichokes, squash, asparagus, sand-dusted mushrooms, mounds of field salad, and deep-purple eggplant, the slender shining aubergine of Provence, were heaped on stall after stall.

An assortment of kitchen knives and mortars and pestles

and olivewood bowls flanked poultry stands of plucked chickens, rabbits, and ducks. Mountainous selections of cheeses breathed in the air. I could never resist the cheeses and the girl behind the counter would slice off a strip of Gruyère for me to taste from a cheese as immense as a yellow marble cornerstone. The streets teamed with women with market baskets, children crowding around the candy bins, men choosing cuts of meat from the butchers. A jaunty musician from Carpentras followed the market from town to town, wheezing his accordion in the din.

On Tuesdays we started out early with every basket and string bag in the house to be filled with the ripe produce of the stalls, each of us, and whoever happened to be visiting, going in a different direction. We would make odd discoveries, and we would often find duplications of pounds of black olives or kilos of *moules* when we met at the Café du Commerce, laden, footsore, and late.

After collapsing in the blue canvas chairs under a parasol, we always ordered cool draughts of beer and watched the market people dismantle their stalls, loading their trucks for the next day's trading in Buis-les-Baronnies, or Valreas, or Malaucène. What tough, handsome, sharp, good-natured people, these gypsies of the marketplace. Bringing their riches of the land to the towns, they banded together in the comradeship of commerce, forever on the road, wanderers of the earth. After enough Tuesday mornings the market vendors came to know us, the Parisians, the Americans, the foreigners, different in our dress, our accents unmarked by the soft Provençal drawl. "Eh, madame, I'll throw in a couple of lemons and some parsley with your trout and red mullets," the brawny blond fishmonger offered after I had hovered too long, fascinated by such deftness and charm, at his crowded stall.

I came to love Tuesday mornings at the market in Vaison-la-Romaine, even though it embodied all the forces conspiring to trap me into becoming a malleable victim of the worshipped Provençal cult of *maîtresse de maison.* I felt my resolve slipping, osmosis taking over. Memory too is a kind of sentimental blackmail. Every time we looked out at the wintry car-packed streets and the steely skyline of New York, we remembered the deep loamed valley of God's Plain. When we roasted a garlicky *gigot* of lamb or smelled the dizzying herbs of a *ratatouille,* visions of La Sérafine rose with the drift. But it was the antiseptic, somnolent, impersonal supermarket that ultimately effected my conversion. Every time I fingered a frozen package of flatulent gray flounder, the image of the handsome, muscular fishmonger and his dappled animals of the sea flashed into focus. A terrible nostalgia engulfed me. I longed to be back wandering in the marketplace of Vaison-la-Romaine. I even longed for the clamor and chaos of my red-tiled kitchen. All ambivalence melted. Could it be that, at last, I had molted from American rebel to docile French *maîtresse de maison?*

FRIENDS AND
NEIGHBORS

Every neighbor is a teacher.

[ARAB PROVERB]

The more we went back to Séguret, the closer we became to the people who had helped us rebuild La Sérafine, and especially to Robert Charrasse, our entrepreneur. Every year there was more work to be done, terraces to be laid, another wing restored, portals for an entrance gate, and Robert prospered along with our house. A go-getter, he was too dynamic, progressive, and ambitious for the small village that contained him. Rather than settling him, success made our handsome young builder restless.

With his wife and two young sons, Robert shared the family house at the foot of the hill. We often stopped by for a *pastis* with them in the garden, or for a game of *boule*. Monsieur André Charrasse, Robert's father, was a champion *bouliste*, a ruddy, blue-eyed man, and, as master mason, titular head of the family enterprise. Both Robert and his younger sister, Josette, had the huge black eyes of their mother, who was the sister of Monsieur Faravel. No doubt the house was too small for comfort, considering that the grandmother who lived with them was ailing, and Robert and his wife expected another child.

As the Charrasse property reached over several acres, enough to accommodate another house, Robert set his masons to work and, by the time the baby arrived, he had moved his family into a fine new villa. Contracts poured in, his business boomed, so Robert invested in another enormous truck and quantities of costly construction equipment. Despite the warnings of his father, he launched many new ventures, including a risky, wide-ranging development of ski lodges on Mont Ventoux, for which he borrowed heavily, overextending his credit with the local banks. Dashing and attractive, Robert liked the good life: partridge shoots, weekends on the Riviera, fine clothes. He took up car racing and traded his Citroën in for a bigger, faster model.

Things went along beautifully for a while and then the crash came. The Charrasse family was dogged by misfortune. It was rumored that the banks threatened to foreclose, which could leave the Entreprise Charrasse in bankruptcy. Shocked and despondent by this turn of events, Monsieur André Charrasse fell ill. The old grandmother died in agony and was buried in the cemetery of Séguret. The front yard of the Charrasse house became another kind of cemetery as masses of equipment rusted and disintegrated, leaving an unsightly dump at the turn-off to our property.

Fortunately, Robert was too resilient and clever to be put down for long. It took a year, but he marshaled his forces, pulling himself out of the red, putting his house back in order. We started him off again by asking him to restore our pavilion and stable into a dining room, kitchen, and library. The ski lodges began to sell as Mont Ventoux became a popular mountain resort. He took up car racing again, paradoxically winning the tortuous course of Mont Ventoux. His family, which for a while had seemed to be hiding behind shutters, blossomed forth and we visited back and forth as usual. Josette Charrasse made a fine marriage to a successful grocer in Vaison-la-Romaine and within two years presented her parents with a new grandson and daughter. Monsieur André Charrasse returned to good health, forbidden so much *pastis* by his doctors, but still able to roll a mean *boule*.

He advised us on the installation of our *boule* court at La Sérafine, and loved to reminisce about his experiences during the war when he hid out in our farmhouse with the maquisards. "Vous savez . . . ce n'etait pas drôle," he would start, telling how our place had been a refuge for the Resistance. He had nearly been devoured by ants while hiding from a Nazi patrol in a clump of bush at the entrance to our road. Robert was just a child then and Josette not yet born. Madame Charrasse lived in terror for fear her husband would be caught and shot. Five members of the Resistance were executed by the Germans in Séguret just before the liberation. "What joy when we saw the Americans come marching down God's Plain!" Monsieur André Charrasse taught us many things about the recent history of our property and we never tired of hearing him spin his stories of our domain. For me, it always came as a surprise to realize that, except for the liberating armies, I was probably the first American to set foot in Séguret and, to my knowledge, the only American resident of the village.

❧

Of all the artisans of Séguret, no one showed a steadier rate of progress than Monsieur Pierre Bonell. As the best electrician and plumber, he had the corner on a growth market. More and more people wanted new kitchens and bathrooms and Monsieur Bonell was the local agent for all the sinks and tubs, washing machines and refrigerators imported to the village. A prudent man, not given to luxuries, he continued to live modestly with his wife and daughters in a simple house in the bend of the road leading up to the Place de la Bise. On Sundays, he and his wife, a very pretty brunette, tended their café in the square, the only one in Séguret, and only open that one day of the week. The Bonell daughters grew up to be both intelligent and good-looking, and one of the girls became a teacher at the primary school of the village.

Without Monsieur Bonell, La Sérafine would never have shone with light; no butane gas would have oozed from the stoves; or water splashed from the taps. Quizzical and determined, at first he balked at my newfangled improvisations, finding it absurd to want three bathrooms and two kitchens, one large and complex for summer when the master chefs perform for a full house of friends, one small and compact for winter when we gather *en famille* in the cozy main wing of La Sérafine. At the beginning he was right; with one paltry well to nourish a fifteen-room house and a waggly electrical extension strung from the Faravel's line, such schemes were, as he claimed, crazy. But now that we have current from L'Électricité de France and water from the Rhône, Monsieur Bonell no longer thinks of me as quite such a *folle Américaine.*

Except for Fraulein Regers, who owned the farmhouse above us and had no such fancy notions, we were the first outlanders to restore a ruin in Séguret. The village, once deserted and as quiet as a tomb, is now a hive of Parisians seeking the sun of Provence. All the old houses have been bought up and are being restored and Monsieur Bonell has never been busier. He has even purchased an eighteenth-century village ruin and is putting it back together as an investment. Considered a magician of modernity, Monsieur Bonell races from place to place doing all sorts of undreamed-of installations, such as burying garden sprinklers and wiring trees with lights. He is literally revolutionizing Séguret and, in the meantime, doing a booming business in water closets and bidets.

Like the village doctor, Monsieur Bonell is always on call. Whenever we arrive at La Sérafine, he bounces up the hill in his small gray truck to say *bonjour.* He knows there are always new things to be done or old things to be fixed. Although he must be extremely well off by now, Monsieur Bonell stays the same: always our good friend, but first of all an expert plumber and electrician, master of his *métiers,* dressed in faded blue workclothes, a jaunty Basque beret perched over one eye.

Friends and Neighbors

I had always harbored a secret *faiblesse* for Gilec Aymard, not just because of his wild ginger hair and green eyes, but because I sensed in him the soul of an artist. He had tooled and crafted all the doors and woodwork at La Sérafine as one, with Pierre Bonell and Robert Charrasse, of the triumvirate of artisans responsible for the restoration of our house. He worked beautifully when the spirit moved him, and not at all when it didn't. I suspected that ordinary functional things, such as the Formica cabinets for our kitchen, bored him, as he took months and months to install them and then never when promised. Carefully carved Provençal cupboards, such as he designed for our linens, on the other hand, always seemed to be finished on time. For the complicated floor-to-ceiling bookshelves in our living room he followed the instructions of Paul-Marc to the letter, just as he fitted fruitwood shelves to the curvy walls of the small library. When we decided, however, to have our hayloft bedroom insulated under pine paneling, the job was shabbily done, the moldings lopped off, the varnish smudged.

It was hard to believe that the same man had done the various jobs. Perhaps Gilec Aymard's assistants were negligent, but I doubt it. I think his perfectionist sense applied only to what interested him, and his pride of accomplishment excluded any but the most exacting and intricate carpentry. As an *ébéniste*, or cabinetmaker, he excelled his *métier* as carpenter. But any workman who gains a reputation as unreliable is quickly classed as *pas sérieux*.

Serious or not, Gilec Aymard prospered as much as his more responsible competitors. When we first arrived in the Vaucluse he had an adequate but hardly extravagant workshop. Now Gilec Aymard works in a massive airy studio with the most modern electrical equipment. We see his name blazoned on the doors as we drive by Sablet on the road back from Carpentras. And even if he took an exceedingly long time to finish our carpentry, as long as it was difficult and of a classical Provençal nature, we knew that eventually we would have an enduring and beautiful piece of craftsmanship. In any case, it was always a pleasure for me to see Gilec Aymard with his curly red hair and roving green eyes.

The foremost antique dealer in Vaison-la-Romaine, Mademoiselle Thérèse Chauvet keeps a dusty, cluttered shop on the rue Jules Ferry. A henna-haired woman with a husky voice and a *Gauloise* stuck to her lower lip, she took a fancy to us because we were friends of Régine Fabre, one of her best clients for Chanteduc, and because of our poodle. Her silver-gray *caniche* romped with Bête-Noire while we poked among the jumble for desks and chairs and chests for our farmhouse in Séguret. Gracefully molded and distinctly Haute-Provence in style, her furniture was *de l'époque*, authentic eighteenth-century Louis Quinze and Louis Seize, or nineteenth-century Louis Philippe and Second Empire. On the pavement flanking her door stood traces from Vaison's Roman digs: fragments, pediments, sawed-off columns, and amphora. Having discovered enough stone remnants on our own property, however, we concentrated on the patina of seasoned wood.

Of course we are always bringing things back from our travels, and gadgets from America, but the objects from our *antiquaire*, Mademoiselle Chauvet, give our *mas* its deeply

Provençal personality. The trough-chested *pétrin* used by housewives for kneading bread, the child's cherrywood spinning wheel, the walnut gloss of the massive armoire in our bedroom. A faded replica of an Aubusson tapestry of the grape-gatherers covers one dining-room wall, and another of the woodcutters hangs above the Louis Treize buffet that Mademoiselle Chauvet brought up in her station wagon. Together we heave and haul the heavy stuff into place, and each year we collect more of her rare and diminishing treasures.

As her antique shop is on the main road into Vaison-la-Romaine, visitors often stop and have things sent to them all over Europe and America. Her cache is being depleted as the demand for Provençal pieces increases. As the country people often put old wood to the fire, some of her grandest armoires lack their classic cornices. At times she is able to salvage merely a pair of doors or a slab of chimney piece, leaving them webby and unpolished in a corner of her back room. The adventure for many collectors, as Mademoiselle Chauvet knows, is discovery; rather than to come upon an object waxed and waiting, it is far more exciting to dig out a wormy coffer deep in dust and time. She also maintains an enviable indifference to commerce, letting rummagers dream-walk for hours among her stock, leave, return, pore over choices or, perhaps, vanish empty-handed. Distinctly out of bounds is haggling, which affronts courtesy in Provence, and Mademoiselle Chauvet dismisses quibblers with a disdainful shrug. If there are any favors to be bestowed she will grant them, often exchanging a dicey find against a better one, or better still, letting our account run carte blanche through the seasons. One day when she invited us to her top-floor apartment, as shining as her shop is shadowy, she let us take the Louis Quinze table right out from under our apéritif glasses.

There are other *antiquaires* who have come to trade in the medieval hill town of Vaison, but none have the stature of Mademoiselle Thérèse Chauvet, indelibly Vaisonnaise and a pillar of the community. She is one of our good friends and every time we elbow through her enthralling muddle we come upon something warm and beautiful and Provençal for the monkish, white-walled rooms of La Sérafine.

We never visited the house of Monsieur Georges Giely, and except through occasional conversations we know very little about him, but he knows quite a lot about us, as he passes by La Sérafine every day when we are there. As our *facteur,* or letter carrier, Monsieur Giely chugs up our hill on his motorbike to deliver village gossip along with the post. A slip of a man with a wide toothless grin and an unshaven chin, he wears a blue beret and the shabbiest clothes of anyone in Séguret. But he has a merry eye and is much stronger than he looks.

Of the two postmen of Séguret, Monsieur Giely has the rural route, which takes him thirty kilometers a day into the back hills, servicing the remote farms of the Commune. Many of the farmers rarely receive a postcard, much less a letter, but they do get a newspaper, one of the Midi dailies—the *Provençal* (Socialist), the *Méridional* (Conservative), the *Dauphiné Libéré* (Socialist), or the *Marseillaise* (Communist)— and Monsieur Giely must deliver these. Although scanty in population, Séguret, in terrain, is among the largest communes in the Vaucluse. Monsieur Giely has a tough route, especially under the scalding summer sun, or when the mistral is at its height in winter, blowing for days at a dizzying gale often reaching fifty kilometers an hour. When Monsieur Giely falls ill, his small brown-haired wife mounts the motorbike and makes his rounds for him.

Even now that we have a fine entrance with wrought-iron grilled gates and a pair of high stone pillars, one of which has a letter slot, Monsieur Giely still comes sauntering bandy-legged down the road with the post. I think he's fascinated by all the international stamps and the people he meets at our kitchen window. He claims we have the most welcoming house of all, always greeting him with a handshake and the offer of a glass of wine. But Monsieur Giely is probably the only man in Séguret who has never accepted a drink, and he has none of the winy glow of the Provençal. "I'm the only sober type in this village," he claims, proudly, "and one of the few loyal Gaullists."

🌹

The gates that Monsieur Giely comes through every morning with the mail were placed at the entrance to La Sérafine by Robert Charrasse, who built the square fieldstone pillars, and by Monsieur Verdeau, who had found the forbidding wrought-iron gates. We were delighted to discover them installed when we arrived for a summer holiday. They added a dimension of Provençal charm and gave us a sense of security. While we were away, Monsieur Verdeau had sometimes surprised people having a Sunday picnic on our terrace, and once he found that our beds had been slept in, probably by a band of gypsies on their way to their big May jamboree in the Camargue.

We asked Monsieur Verdeau where he had found such a handsome pair of gates, neither too high nor too low, but just in scale to the clean, strong lines of our farmhouse. He told us they had been the entrance gates to a property near his, a place that had once belonged to an Englishwoman. This piqued my curiosity, as I had thought of myself as the only Anglo-Saxon resident of Séguret. One night I asked Madame Verdeau to tell me more about this Englishwoman, whose gates now guarded our place.

Madame Verdeau told me that when she and her husband had moved into their family house shortly after their marriage, they had for neighbors the unlikely couple of a young Englishwoman and her Provençal lover. It seemed that she, a certain Miss Leslie, was older than he, but richer. She owned the house and her jewels were the talk of the village. Theirs was a love-hate relationship, and the Verdeaus could not help but overhear their quarrels, which were frequent and mostly about money. After one particularly tumultuous night, Miss Leslie vanished.

The lover, a brutish if handsome man, went about explaining that Miss Leslie had received an urgent cable calling her home. She had left by early morning bus for the Avignon train to Calais and on across the Channel to England. This story was accepted by the villagers for some time, although no letters with British stamps arrived for Miss Leslie's Provençal fiancé. Naturally the postman mentioned this odd fact on his rounds. People began to talk. After a year had gone by, Miss Leslie's lover told Madame Verdeau, in a fit of weeping, that Miss Leslie had decided to stay in England. A few months later he married and brought his bride to live in the house.

Although the people of Séguret disapproved of this behavior, his actions would have remained unquestioned, had not a member of the secret police based in Avignon taken a weekend house near Miss Leslie's former villa. The neighbors whispered rumors of the strange departure of the Englishwoman, arousing the suspicions of the agent to such an extent that he began an investigation. The secret agent took his time, training a telescope on the house, watching the movements of his suspect.

It took several years of questioning the villagers to find no confirmation of Miss Leslie's having been on the bus on the said morning to Avignon. In Orange, the telegraph office had no duplicate of the cable summoning her back to England. Furthermore, at Avignon, the railroad clerk could trace no reservation in her name for the train to Calais and the channel boat produced no record of her crossing. Most damaging of all, Interpol's British agents turned up not a shred of information as to Miss Leslie's whereabouts in England. In other words, there was not the slightest evidence that Miss Leslie had ever left Séguret.

This convinced the secret agent of the man's guilt. One winter morning he struck at dawn with a team of detectives, entering the house, shaking the suspect awake and shouting, "Where is the body?" As if startled from a nightmare the man answered, "Under the chicken coop, near the garage." Forcing him out of bed, they shoved a pick into his hands. "Dig up the floor or we'll pull down the garage." Sweating, stripped to the waist, the man hacked at the frozen earth until he uncovered most of the fetid bones of Miss Leslie. Her head was never found.

After his confession, knowing he was doomed, the man took his own life by slashing his wrists, and died in the prison of Avignon.

This scandal gave the villa a bad name, and then, too, there was a good deal of litigation before the place could be sold again. Finally, some Parisians had bought the house and decided to change the entrance. Finding the gates just right for us, Monsieur Verdeau had acquired them for La Sérafine, and we embellished the pillars with statues of Pan and Bacchus. Now, when the shutters bang on a windless night, or a mirror suddenly crashes to the floor, I wonder if it is not the spirit of Miss Leslie coming back to haunt us, but Monsieur Verdeau shrugs off these omens merely as the result of the sonic boom of jets based in Orange.

We never managed to become friends with two of our closest neighbors. One family, the Girards, are among the richest people in Séguret. The other family, the Martins, are among the poorest. We see the properties of both families every day, but rarely the people. Both houses, each in its own way, are beautiful, contained, Provençal, and unapproachable.

The Girard place is hidden from view by the copse of pines on our western flank, but we passed the great walled manor house every time we drove up the road to La Sérafine. On a lap of land between the Faravel and the Charrasse properties, it stands back from the road, shielded by an avenue of cypress trees, barred by a rose-covered gate, forever locked. Our district of Saint-Jean takes its name from their private baroque chapel, as visible as the house is hidden, a landmark crowning a mound of pines. One day our friend Roger Fabre took us to call. The Girards were polite, showing us around the gardens, romantic with urns of pink geraniums and flights of fantailed pigeons, cool with fountains and secret glades. The house had belonged to Maurice Constantin, a relative of Madame Girard and a famous French writer. It was he who restored the chapel on the hill and marked the house with his romanticism. A faint melancholy still hung over the great tiled rooms in spite of the distinct lack of romanticism of Monsieur and Madame Girard. Except for their immediate family, they rarely received visitors. They never encouraged us to pursue this introduction, and in all the years we have been neighbors we have seen the Girards perhaps twice on the road. They never returned our call.

Dappled in mauve shadows, its sepia roof slanted over rough stones, the Martin house stands on our eastern flank, a tawny peasants' dwelling cradled in the saddle of a hill. Called La Jas, a cut in size above a *mas,* we see it framed in all of our south-facing windows, a perfect Cézanne caught in time and space.

We wanted to meet the Martins, but Monsieur Faravel dissuaded us. He told us strange stories about them. How their wild daughter ran in the woods like an untamed gazelle. How fiercely they resented us as outsiders restoring the only place in the Commune more impoverished than their own. They resented our intrusion, tilling fields on the border of their land, encroaching on their privacy, exposing the dark hillside of their misery to the eyes of the world. Occasionally, we heard their donkey braying, but we never saw a light in the house, nor smoke rising from the chimney.

Sometimes I have walked through our vineyard to the edge

of their land, hoping to meet Monsieur and Madame Martin or their legendary daughter. I felt I might overcome their hostility by assuring them of our goodwill. Most of all, I longed to thank them for never changing one stone of the perfect sculpture that meets my eyes every waking morning at La Sérafine. But the Martins, like the north side of their house, turn their backs to us.

Our dearest, most trusted, and oldest friends in Séguret were Monsieur and Madame Lucien Faravel. Without their guidance and confidence, their loyalty and protection, we would never have found, much less finished, our farmhouse in Provence. As our closest neighbors they acted as guardian angels of La Sérafine, keeping out intruders but welcoming friends who sometimes used the house when we were not there. They particularly liked our American friends for their effervescence and generosity, and our friends never forgot the Faravels, without whom La Sérafine might have seemed hostile and alien.

Although a native of Séguret, Monsieur Faravel was considered a prodigal son returned from the big city with a Parisian wife. To their sorrow, the Faravels were childless, which made life in the country lonely. In addition, matters of inheritance and the division of the family property caused friction with Monsieur Faravel's relatives, the Charrasse family. Our restoring of La Sérafine had been a boon to the Faravels, bringing them in touch with the outside world. By the same token, the Faravels had been a boon to us, keeping us in touch with the world of Séguret. When we were in Séguret we

were always together, and when away, always in correspondence. One letter from Madame Faravel brought the exciting
news of an expected child. Naturally we cabled our congratula-
tions immediately, adding the traditional Provençal good
wishes that their child be "as wise as salt, as true as bread, as
full as an egg, and as straight as a matchstick." Sylvie, a
brown-eyed baby girl, arrived when we were at La Sérafine,
and much to our delight, Paul-Marc was asked to be her god-
father, her *parrain,* not a small honor or responsibility in
France.

Sylvie grew to be plump and beautiful in the sun of Provence. She was closely guarded, petted and admonished in
equal measure, an imaginative child used to the company of
her dolls, her parents, and the television. For the Faravels, the
world revolved around Sylvie. They planned for her school-
ing, her future, and probably feared for her inheritance.
Monsieur Faravel, in his fifties, was a good deal older than his
wife and his only capital was his property, still a matter of family dispute. Madame Faravel, delicate, sensitive, always a
bit *fatiguée,* was never really happy in the country even
though her mother visited often, keeping a room furnished
with her own things at the Faravels'.

The summer of Sylvie's fourth year, Madame Faravel became really *fatiguée* because her mother had decided to settle
in the Mediterranean town of Hyères. I had seen Madame
Faravel weeping and distraught as the movers hauled out
the chest and bed and chairs and packed them in the big blue
van. Hyères was merely a few hours' drive away and actually
brought her mother closer than she had been in Paris, but
the gesture was a wrench for Madame Faravel. Monsieur
Faravel went about chatting and gossiping with the neigh-

bors, but Madame Faravel clung to Sylvie and stayed closer and closer to home.

The next time we went to La Sérafine, as usual we honked the horn as we approached the tall pair of cypress trees leading to the Faravel property. We swerved into their drive, but the iron gates were closed. There was no car in the garage, no sign of Sylvie's tricycle, no metal table under the willow in the graveled courtyard, no plastic streamers flapping at the kitchen door. The pale-blue shutters were barred and all the ducks and chickens gone. An eerie silence hung over this house usually so full of sights and sounds. The Faravels must be away visiting Madame Faravel's mother in Hyères, we decided, heading up the hill to our house.

In the dining room we found a letter propped against a vase of flowers. "Chers Amis," Madame Faravel began. "We had to make a grave decision, to sell the house for various reasons and very quickly. I know this will make you very unhappy but we hope always to keep your affection as you have been our only true friends in Séguret, the only ones we could really count on. Please understand, chers amis, it caused us deep sorrow to leave Séguret, but there have been too many troubles with the family. . . . Sylvie must start school this fall and we feel that for her sake it would be better here. We have bought an apartment in Hyères, three rooms, kitchen, hall, w.c., with a view of the old town and the sea. We hope for the joy of receiving you soon. You will always have a welcome place at our table. . . . There we are, chers amis, our news is sad, but we had to do it. Meantime we beg you to accept our long and affectionate friendship. Sylvie sends kisses."

The letter as usual was signed "toutes nos amitiés, A. Faravel." Was it an A or a D or a G? I couldn't make it out.

In all the years of our binding friendship, it was not until Madame Faravel had left Séguret that I realized I had never known her first name.

The Faravels sold their house and land to Monsieur Marcel Augier, the son-in-law of our aloof neighbor Monsieur Girard. It happened suddenly. The Augiers, who lived in Vaison-la-Romaine, decided to build a summer house four miles south in Séguret. They tore down the ruined farmhouse on the southern rim of the copse of pines across from the Girard mansion and started constructing an enormous modern Provençal house. As Monsieur Augier owned a company of building materials, everything was of the best quality. Money was no object and eventually he counted on embellishing his place with a swimming pool. All he lacked was water, which the Faravels had in abundance from a source in the hills behind their house. Monsieur Augier bought the package deal: spring, pines, vineyard, orchards, and the house, in which he lodged transient construction workers. This ensured him, not only of sufficient water, but of privacy. Now no one, especially not Robert Charrasse, whose family property it had been, could blemish the landscape with a complex of holiday villas.

We were deeply saddened by the departure of the Faravels. The sprig of willow that Monsieur Faravel had planted from his tree in our courtyard grew from a plume to a fountain of feathery branches. Somehow it symbolized our friendship with the Faravels, a friendship we felt would continue to grow in spite of distance. We wrote to them at their new address: Residence Beethoven No. 3. How contrived and ordinary and anonymous it sounded for Monsieur and Madame Lucien Faravel, landed gentry of the Quartier Saint-Jean of

Séguret. We hoped to drive to Hyères to see them and invited them to visit us or at least spend a holiday at La Sérafine after we left. But the Faravels never came. They once saw the Verdeau family on their way through Séguret, but they didn't go to La Sérafine. To reach our place they would have to pass the property that was no longer theirs. Monsieur Faravel was having difficulty adjusting to life in a three-room apartment in a crowded and noisy resort town. He could not yet bring himself to mount the hillside and behold the vines and the pines and the house of his childhood, the house where he had planned to end his days. The wounds were still too raw, the remorse too deep to endure the humiliation of accepting the decay of his family seat, reduced in a few months to a lifeless hulk, unloved and abandoned to time.

The Verdeau family opened up a whole new vista of life for us in Séguret. Our main contacts had been with the artisans of the village, the Charrasse family, our entrepreneurs, and the Faravels, our good friends and guardians. For the first time we were in close touch with people of the land, *agriculteurs,* who earned their livelihood ploughing and sowing, reaping and marketing their harvests. Monsieur Verdeau was a hard-working farmer, *un homme sérieux,* in the fields from dawn until dusk, in contrast to Monsieur Faravel, who was considered more of a gentleman farmer. In character, the two men were poles apart.

Whereas Monsieur Faravel was very *bavard,* loquacious and confidential, Monsieur Verdeau was tight-lipped and skeptical, his observations a mixture of distrust, discretion, and wry humor. Monsieur Faravel waved his arms expansively, shrugged, talked compulsively on every subject, almost embracing his listener as a torrent of words poured from his lips. Monsieur Verdeau dropped phrases from the corner of his mouth with distance and reserve. Even in his workclothes, Monsieur Faravel had a certain chic. Although older, Monsieur Faravel looked softer, his skin smooth beside the weathered brow of Monsieur Verdeau, whose skin was browned and taut over his strong nose and jutting jaw. Sweat glistened in his curled hair. His handclasp had the grip of a rock and he smiled without baring his teeth. In his forties, Jean Verdeau had the bent of a man who had grappled with the land, the muscle of a tiller, and the eye of a falcon stooping his prey.

At first I found Monsieur Verdeau distant and austere, having been so used to the warmth and ebullience of the Faravels. But Paul-Marc, who got along well with all the villagers, had immediate rapport with Jean Verdeau. They both understood the language of the land. Season by season, our friendship with the Verdeau family grew, becoming deeper as our vineyards flourished, and more enduring as our orchards flowered. Our mutual respect was rooted in the earth we shared. Monsieur and Madame Verdeau often invited us for an apéritif at their house, where we sat under a garden trellis of white jasmine and drank a tumbler of *rosé* wine. Usually, we went about seven in the evening, when the light darkened and the family had returned from gathering the fruits. Everyone worked, starting at sunrise, stopping for lunch, bringing in the last tractor at sunset. Madame Verdeau, tall and straight with velvety brown eyes, looked cool in her simple blue dress. Of the three Verdeau daughters, only Giselle, at seven, was too young for the harvest. She had the great brown eyes of her mother, a slight, sweet little girl with black hair. Simone, seventeen, round and dark, and Michèle, eighteen, slim and fair, worked all day with their parents and their older brother, Jean-Pierre, who handled the tractor like a toy. He was twenty, tall and brawny, his broad chest bronzed, his thick brown hair matted in curls. Having studied agriculture in Avignon, he decided, unlike most of the young men of Séguret, to stay and work the land with his father.

The Verdeau house looked enormous, two stories of fieldstone with wings and annexes to the rear and an entrance of tall portals screened by high grilled gates. An alley of chestnut trees led to the courtyard where Madame Verdeau kept chickens and ducks in pens. A garden of roses and gladioli and geraniums faced the graveled terrace off the dining room. The house belonged to her family, who had lived in Séguret and the neighboring villages for generations. Monsieur Verdeau was not *du pays,* but half Belgian and half Lyonnais, with all the sturdy, dependable characteristics of those regions. They had met and married during the war, when Monsieur Verdeau had been stationed at the air base in Orange. In the city of Lyons, his father was a merchant, and he had been educated by the Jesuit fathers. Jean Verdeau preferred, however, to settle in the country of his wife, and bring up his family in Séguret.

Monsieur Verdeau was master of many trades: vintner, carpenter, electrician, mechanic, forger, and gardener. He was also deeply involved in the affairs of Séguret, and had a strong voice in politics, voting firmly to the Left. He shared the farmers' grievances of too low prices for producers and too high profits for the middlemen. He voted for the party that he believed would bring progress to the village. Although not a stalwart member of the parish, his children were baptized in the Church and would be married there.

The Verdeau children married young. Jean-Pierre was barely twenty-one when he chose his wife, a strong, vivacious Italian girl whose family had come from the Piedmont to settle as farmers in the plain of Séguret. The tallest and most handsome young man in the village, Jean-Pierre might easily have won the hand of one of the pretty, blond, and richly dowered daughters of the prosperous baker, but he chose to marry for love. He and Marisa spent a wintry honeymoon in Rome before coming back to set up housekeeping in their own place on the Route of the Princes of Orange. It was a small family house, made cozy and comfortable by Jean-Pierre and his father who had worked all year getting it ready, paneling the ceilings, troweling the walls, installing a modern bathroom and kitchen. Rows of pear trees shielded the garden, and in the distance high green hills rose to the sky. Jean-Pierre continued working the land with his father and took an extra job at the wine cooperative, so he and Marisa could buy a small car and a large television. Within a year their daughter, Sabine, was born, and the following year, their son, Eric. Everyone considered them an ideal Provençal *ménage,* young, hard-working, and *très sérieux.*

The oldest Verdeau daughter, Michèle, married at nineteen. It was a love match and a very good one, as her young man owned sixteen hectares of splendid vineyards and a fine house, Le Clos des Chênes, set among towering oak trees beside a riverlet on the outskirts of Vaison-la-Romaine. Mademoiselle Verdeau marrying Monsieur Plantevin seemed especially apt and might be translated as Mademoiselle Glass-of-

Water becoming Madame Plant-the-Vines. Michèle had much the same arrangement as her mother, pens of chickens and ducks, a garden of flowers, and a beautiful big kitchen in which to receive her friends. Her husband, Lucien, with blond hair and slate-blue eyes, had the strong hands of a vintner. Two Spanish workers who lived on the property helped him with the vineyards. By the time she was twenty, Michèle was the radiant mother of a bouncing son, Jean-Marc, who looked, in his magnificent big pram, a miniature of his blond and blue-eyed father.

Simone Verdeau, a year younger than Michèle, met a vibrant and intelligent young Italian in Jonquières, the town where her grandmother lived. He had a good job at the atomic installation of Pierrelatte and a small Renault station wagon. After a springtime courtship, they announced their engagement, but the housing shortage in Jonquières prevented their marrying for a year. Finally, when they found a pretty little place with a garden, Simone Verdeau and Laurent Tovena were married in the Church of Saint-Denis in Séguret. Within a year, they presented the Verdeaus with another grandchild, Isabelle. Simone loves being a housewife and a mother, after having spent her adolescence harvesting the grapes and picking the fruits with her parents. For Laurent, cooped up in an office all day, the *vendange* counts as a holiday and at the time of the harvest, he strips off his shirt and joins the grape-gatherers, happy to be out in the blazing sun.

Monsieur and Madame Verdeau consider themselves fortunate in having the young people so near. Their youngest daughter, Giselle, plays with the babies as if they were dolls, and every Sunday there is a family reunion at the big house.

We are often invited and it is wonderful to know such a family, to share their happiness, and to feel their love.

There is never a shadow of a doubt as to who is the head of the Verdeau clan. It is Jean Verdeau, sometimes stern and close-fisted, always a solid provider, and, for the most part, an indulgent despot. Curiously, the generation gap seems not to have rent this family's ranks. The children revere their father and confide in their mother. The girls, rather than rebel by veering toward a more bourgeois way of life, have followed their mother's custom of inviting people to share the warmth of their kitchens for a glass of wine, and of course the kitchens of young Provençaux *ménages* today are very well equipped. They all have television, too, a diversion still scorned by the family patriarch. Emotionally close-knit and fiercely loyal, the Verdeau tribe sticks together, works together, and sees as much of each other as possible. They appear to be marvelously content with their lot, which indeed improves every year.

XIV

6,000 BOTTLES
OF WINE

*Oh, for a beaker full
of the warm South . . .
With beaded bubbles
winking at the brim . . .*

[KEATS, "Ode to a Nightingale"]

Summer after summer we marveled at the miracle of our land
as the undulating slopes turned from grubby brown to a
broadloom of tender green. The first tendrils pushed up in
little clumps like lonely pale lettuces in too vast a bed. Under
the magnanimous sun of the Vaucluse and the gentle prod-
ding of Monsieur Verdeau, they soon became vines, stretching, reaching for the sky, their arms jeweled in lucent leaves.
To give them air and light, Jean-Pierre Verdeau strung ribbons of wire, taming, training the branches to interlock until

their leaves entwined wave after wave of vines dancing an eternal ballet to the music of the wind. Finally, we saw the first waxen fruits in golden clusters on the branches and Monsieur Verdeau assured us that in the autumn our vineyard would yield its first grapes for wine.

"The grapes are bursting on the vines . . . a fantastic year for the Rhône Valley wines, you must come for the vendange," Monsieur Verdeau wrote with unaccustomed verve, urging us to drop everything and fly to Séguret to harvest our vineyards. There was a shortage of labor and our grapes, as the best in Séguret, had been left to mellow in the sun until their juice ran with the highest degree of alcohol. Most of the vineyards had been stripped before October, but ours, curved as they were around an amphitheater of hillside facing south, could risk an extra week of sun. Our wine would be only of the *cuvée des gourmets,* of the top quality. What a celebration! But how could we manage it? July had been our month in the country, a hard-won vacation, and our only one at La Sérafine.

Monsieur Verdeau's ebullient letter, however, spurred my imagination. What a splendid idea to have a reunion of the entire family for our first great *vendange.* It was, after all, the culmination of our dream, the victory of the land, the triumph of La Sérafine, to be plucking our first purple fruits, to watch the blood of our grapes flow into vats to age for our first heady wine. On the spur of the moment, I decided to fly over for the grape harvest. I sent a flurry of cables all over the world. Beau-Père could take the train from Bayonne to Avignon. Jacques and Nicole had not yet started classes and could drive down from Paris. Paul-Marc was on mission in Kenya en route to Rome, where friends would motor him up to Provence. My sister Peggy, in Madrid, would be putting her girls into Marymount School in Barcelona and could meet me in Marseilles. I took the Air France night flight from New York and joined her at Marignane airport, where we were met by Monsieur Verdeau.

It had been raining and cold in New York, but the air was as soft as silk in Provence. At Salon, the first welcoming bower of plane trees branched over the main street and we stopped in the shadow of the bronze figure of Nostradamus. I had spotted an irresistible market and was aching to finger the glossy aubergines and bite into a warm, ripe Provençal tomato. The produce was set out in baskets, a marvelous still life of green peppers, watercress, pink-and-white radishes, gritty mushrooms, lemons, yellow onions, and mounds of field salad, *la doucette,* as the Provençaux call it. Inside, where chandeliers of garlic hung and buckets of black olives shone, we heaped up a carton of food.

October is the oyster season, so we stocked up on a supply and bought a knife to open them. Boursin with *fines herbes,* chèvre, and Caprices des Dieux were our cheeses. At the butcher we found white veal and a *gigot* of three pounds, and at the bakery, two wands of bread and a bag of butter croissants. Doing the *marché* made us feel we were really back in Provence.

In Séguret, Madame Verdeau, Beau-Père, and Simone were waiting for us at the Verdeau house. Monsieur Verdeau had paved his graveled terrace with flagstones and bought new blue deck chairs and there we chatted as though we had never been away. Jacques called to say he had been held up by an exam in Paris and, as Paul-Marc would not arrive until the following day, Monsieur Verdeau lent us a 1950 Deux Chevaux, which I ground and bounced and urged up the hill to the house.

We got our bags and groceries inside, and after changing we walked down to have a look at the vines. Indeed, they were bent and heavy with grapes, great clusters weighing down every branch. We plucked a basket for the house, some of the tawny pink grapes for the rosé wine and some of the deep purple for the red. They were sweet and warm from the sun and tasted delicious after the feast of oysters we had on the terrace.

On the horizon we could see dark clouds forming and by nightfall ominous peals of thunder cracked the sky. A fearful storm was brewing. Streaks of lightning lit up the valley and suddenly we heard a great barrage of gunfire, as though God's Plain were being bombed. Small bursts of orange flashed against the black clouds. I rushed to our new telephone to ask Monsieur Verdeau what was happening, but he assured me all was normal. Séguret owned seventeen bazookas, which were fired into threatening skies to break up the hail, far more dangerous to the vines than rain. Thunder and lightning and the barrage went on and on. Hoping against hope, we prayed for Paul-Marc to arrive. I had never seen our dulcet sun-streaked valley struck by more than a vigorous master wind and this angry sky worried me. We brought in logs from the cave in the guesthouse and lit a fire in the library. Beau-Père went about battening down the blinds, mumbling Ave Maria's, calling on lost saints remembered. "Après nous, le déluge," he exclaimed as a gust of wind hurled him through the French doors and the rain suddenly came down in rivers.

The storm was fierce, too driving for us to go outside and

close the kitchen shutters. We could see the forks of lightning splitting the heavens as we gathered around the stove nervously slicing the aubergines, peppers, onions, and tomatoes for a *ratatouille*. One of my favorite and most accomplished dishes, it is something I always resort to cooking in moments of stress. We kept our spirits up by singing and gulping down goblets of gold-medal red. From time to time the lights went out after an especially loud slap of thunder and we scurried for the butt ends of candles left over from the summer. Just as we lit them the electricity returned. As we were about to settle at the table, we noticed the kitchen tiles sinking in water, which rose with alarming speed, so that all the kitchen-floor rags and sponges we applied failed to stem the flow. We were beginning to panic when Beau-Père decided there must be an unseen leak. By pulling out the refrigerator, we discovered a stream of water gushing in from a hole the size of a tennis ball. We plugged it with an empty wine bottle and disconnected the flimsy extension cord to which the refrigerator, for some inexplicable reason, was attached. Then the lights went dead as a bolt of blinding lightning flashed, thunder roared on its heels, and we knew the storm was right on top of us. We crowded into a corner near the doorway together as the house was struck. A ball of fire, glistening, yellow, rolled in from the open circuit, danced over the red tiles by our feet, careened through the entrance hall and out the door. We were paralyzed with fear; acrid smoke filled the air.

"The house is on fire," Peggy screamed. Thank God she's alive, I thought, dashing to douse the flaming dust cloths under the sink. Thunder, lightning, wind, and rain howled about the house. The entire countryside was plunged in darkness. The *ratatouille* was still bubbling on the gas stove. We lit the candles and settled down at the long shadowy table—a white-haired patriarch with two trembling women. Out of hysteria and terror, we ate ravenously, overcome with relief and at our good fortune to be alive. The peals of thunder began to come at longer intervals after the streaks of lightning and we knew the storm was subsiding. The rain still fell, washing the roof above our heads as we crawled into bed, leaving the doors open between the rooms, spent with fear and fatigue and the foreboding that the storm had cut our grapes from their stems or reduced our wine to water.

The next morning when Paul-Marc arrived with our friends, we investigated the damage. The plug of the telephone was in the washing machine, every light bulb had fragmented to bits, and the stainless-steel sink had been ripped by the ball of fire. Monsieur Bonell came up to say that the Girards, the Augiers, the Faravel house, in fact everyone on our hillside, had been struck by lightning. The hole in the wall from which the water gushed had been my fault. He had left it for my dishwasher, that hypothetical mechanical helper that would never arrive. All the telephone wires were down. What concerned us most, however, were the vines.

The storm had been a disaster for the vintners with vineyards in the plain. Paul-Marc and I rushed down to the cooperative as Monsieur Lebrun was bringing his grapes, soggy, and reduced to eight degrees. In town, everyone was talking weather. The fine new shelter of reeding over the tables of the Café du Commerce had blown down. Next door, the awning of the café that advertised "baby-foot," a pinball game of football, had crumpled. Everyone was praying for a good cold whip of the mistral, a wind that blows away clouds and illness, *un vent sain,* a healthy wind, as they say in Provence.

We expected Monsieur Verdeau to be in despair because of the storm but he showed his usual *sang-froid.* The rains had rolled off our rocky hillside like water off a swan's neck, he assured us, and we had better all be up and in the vineyards at six the next morning.

It was my turn to feel like Marie Antoinette at her *petit hameau.* We set the alarm and got up at daybreak. By the time we had coffee and arrived at the vineyards, Monsieur Verdeau was there with his orange tractor and his team of *vendangeurs.* Simone worked fastest and best, like a round dark gypsy in her pale-blue smock. She had been picking fruits and grapes since the age of fourteen. "C'est dur," she said, lopping off bunch after bunch of Grenache grapes with her sharp knife. There were others working too: Benoit, a young Spaniard of sixteen whose father had settled in the region; Claude, whose father owned the nursery where we bought our plants and shrubs; Jean-Pierre Verdeau, handsome and strong, who picked grapes until eight, when he went to work at the cooperative for the rest of the day.

I had brought gardening scissors for our team and Monsieur Verdeau provided us with plastic buckets. Each cluster had about fifty grapes, Monsieur Verdeau explained, as he taught us how to snip the largest number of bunches in the quickest possible time. You hold the clump of grapes in your left hand, cut with the right, and drop the fruit into the bucket in a kind of one-two-three movement. When the bucket is filled, you take it to the tractor and throw the grapes into a larger vat which is heaved into a trailer to be carted to the cooperative.

6,000 Bottles of Wine

Our first load weighed well over a ton, and Monsieur Verdeau drove it down to the entrance to the cooperative. After he had dumped the grapes into a huge grinder, Madame Estève, the wife of the superintendent, tested the juice in a refractometer for the degree of sugar and alcoholic content. Our first batch read eleven degrees, which meant it would come to twelve. The grapes were then pressed. The wine is stored in concrete vats to age for the *vin ordinaire,* but for the *cuvée des gourmets,* such as ours, it rests in huge oaken vats, marked five thousand litres. The vats are enormous, planted on stands in a huge cave, reeking of wine. Bronze plaques mark the year: 1982—14°. When we went to the room of the *dégustation,* Jean-Pierre was there offering us the best of the cave in small round glasses.

Everyone took special pride in the *dégustation,* because our wine had just achieved the honor of a village classification. No longer would the wine of the cooperative of Roaix-Séguret have merely an *appellation* Côtes-du-Rhônes. We were now *vignerons,* with a special label, one equal in quality to that of Tavel or Gigondas. This merit had been bestowed because the wines of Roaix-Séguret had won a silver and a gold medal at the Paris Fair of Vintners; a grand prize, a gold medal, and two first prizes at Mâcon; a gold medal at Orange; and a silver medal at Brignoles.

In order to achieve the privilege of *vignerons,* proof of the long history of plantation had to be presented. As vice-president of the cooperative, Monsieur Verdeau had helped unearth the document in the Inguimbert Library in Carpentras dating from 1746, stating that Séguret and Roaix had always grown vines of superior quality. Now the brochures read, "Les Vignerons de Roaix-Séguret vous offrent leurs 'Côtes-du-Rhônes' Rosés," agreeable, nervous, and subtle, and "leurs 'Côtes-du-Rhônes' rouges," aged in oak, heady, full-bodied with delicate bouquet.

As members of the cooperative we were entitled to a special *tarrif,* but even for consumers all over France, or the world, the price for the best gold medal was about ninety cents a bottle, and as little as forty cents for the lesser vintages.

Jacques and Nicole arrived and we all worked in the vineyards from morn until night for three days. Beau-Père wore a straw hat against the sun and had his special system, which made him a champion. From the top of the slope, Jacques communicated by walkie-talkie with Nicole, who wore a bikini to renew her suntan as a *vendangeuse.* I loved being a grape-gatherer. The sun shone down hot and strong, and my back ached from bending over the vines, but the air glistened and the sky opened blue and clear above. We were all working together and there was a wonderful spirit of comradeship.

We planned a party celebrating the final day of our grape-gathering. Everyone climbed the hill to the terrace, all of us hot and tired and strangely exhilarated, for no matter how arduous the labor of the *vendange,* it is, above all, a labor of love. It is the *raison d'être* of the village of Séguret, and there is not one villager who does not rejoice in a good harvest. At dinner, there were exuberant toasts and teary speeches, unprecedented outbursts of emotion for the reserved Provençaux, as we congratulated each other on the success of the season. For the Verdeau family and for us, the *vendange* sealed a bond, confirming our future, crystallizing our friendship as partners irrevocably rooted in the same land. Monsieur Verdeau lifted his glass ceremoniously, praising the yield of our property, sixty hectoliters of wine from six tons of grapes. We were delirious with joy. At last we counted as true citizens of Séguret with our own *cru*. The cellars of the Clos de La Sérafine overflowed. We could drown in *rosé* and *rouge*. Our vineyards had produced six thousand bottles of wine!

XV

LOVE AND
A VINEYARD

In this valley
closed about on all sides . . .
pensive and with slow steps,
I walk with my love.

[PETRARCH]

More than an achievement, going to the grape harvest marked
a milestone, especially for me. On his United Nations mis-
sions abroad, Paul-Marc often managed to slip down to
Provence for a weekend to confer on the new constructions
with Robert Charrasse and look over the property with Jean
Verdeau. He would enjoy only a glimpse, not a real holiday,
but at least it provided him a link with La Sérafine, which,
for me, remained frustratingly elusive. Having our country
house an ocean away sometimes seemed an absurd extrava-

gance, or, as Beau-Père predicted, *une grande folie.* Too distant for Christmas or Easter vacations, La Sérafine served us only one fleeting month out of twelve. We were forever caught between memory and desire, nostalgic for summers past, longing for summers to come. "Last year . . . next year . . ." was our constant and plaintive refrain, and when friends asked, "How much time can you spend there?" the once-a-year response sounded faintly ridiculous. For the first time, I could honestly answer: in July to pick the apricots and in October to gather the grapes.

Climbing back from the vineyards, we realized the enchanting pleasance our front orchard formed in relation to the house. A shaggy carpet of green had begun to sprout around the peach and plum trees from the Kentucky Blue Grass and Ruf-Tuf seed we sent over for Monsieur Verdeau to sow. Although we looked down at the little orchard from the terrace, we rarely went there except to gather a basket of fruit. What a splendid place for a swimming pool, we decided, and asked Robert Charrasse to draft a design. Robert suggested a basin, something rustic and pragmatic, at once a pool and an irrigation source for our vineyards. In that way, it would count as part of the farm rather than a flagrant sign of taxable affluence—*un signe extérieur de richesse.*

Naturally, our first practical plan for an irrigation basin grew to far more lavish proportions. We stepped off the space with Robert Charrasse, and rather than a rim of lawn decided on a flagstone deck for sunning. In that case, a flight of fieldstone steps should lead from the west entrance and a graded path from the east terrace under the lime tree. Instead of a pond large enough to cool off in we enlarged the dimensions to ten meters by seven. Then we decided it should be at least two meters deep. As that meant a day to empty the pool, a day to clean it, and a day to refill it, the only sane thing would be to have a filter. How heavenly to look down at the garden and see running water! So we asked Robert to design a fountainhead and Monsieur Bonell to install an underwater light.

Being so close to the sea we had always thought it a lark to drive an hour for a dip in the Mediterranean. We had gone only a few times, however, finding the coast so thronged with cars and the pebbly sands so swarming with oiled bodies that we rushed back to the silence and serenity of La Sérafine. Water changed everything. We no longer depended on our meager well. Now, with the welcome flow from the Rhône, we could have our own private Côte d'Azur—a magnificent, deep, rippling, lighted swimming pool.

Robert broke ground before the winter snows, and poured tons of reinforced concrete into the rectangular hole after the spring frosts. Monsieur Verdeau wrote, giving us news of the bulbs we had planted in the autumn, at the time of the grape harvest. People from all over the countryside were coming to see our tulips . . . "so magnificent, so brilliant in color that everyone thinks they're plastic."

In addition to being our vintner and our new guardian, Monsieur Verdeau had become *Le Nôtre* of La Sérafine. Not just his thumbs, all of his ten fingers proved to be green, and whereas vineyards and orchards were his domain, Madame Verdeau knew all about flowers. She advised him on the garden, choosing a variety of roses, the deep-red Sangria and Fire Dance bushes to contrast with the bright pinks of the Champs-Élysées. Against the north wall of the house, she seeded Marguerites that grew as tall as shrubs, their white-enameled petals spoking from hubs of yellow velvet. For the courtyard, they transplanted geraniums, which spilled in scarlet profusion over the rim of the ocher stone oatbin.

"Les jardins sont riants de fleurs," Monsieur Verdeau wrote exuberantly. For him to resort to such vivid metaphor must mean that the garden really was a riot of color, laughing with flowers.

When we arrived at La Sérafine in June, silken red poppies specked the fields and clumps of broom exploded yellow on the hills. Monsieur and Madame Verdeau greeted us at the house and led us out to the terrace. We could hardly believe our eyes. Below, the new swimming pool shimmered, a huge aquamarine mounted in emerald-green grass, bordered by trees of pink-gold apricots. A hedge of cypresses lined the lane to the new vineyard gate, and the hill of rubble under the lime tree blazed in red geraniums. Monsieur Verdeau had re-designed the orchard as a classical French formal garden, cut-ting paths of raked gravel among the flower beds, banking the plots of roses with walls of stone. From the courtyard, the willow branches cascaded over the wall to climbing rose-bushes and a legion of flaming gladioli.

Our packets of sunflower seeds from California took root and thrived in Provence, forming a small forest, their giant blond heads nodding against the navy-blue sky. Madame Verdeau showed me the Roman trough, now blooming with a mixture of flat enameled petals called *les porcelaines* and sproutings of *mères de familles,* aptly named, as they repro-duce so profusely. All the thick, tortuous thornbush had been hacked from the well, leaving the stones exposed, so that it looked like an immense hive under the bee-loud lime blossoms. Behind it, Monsieur Verdeau carved a path bordering it in ban-ners of mauve and white petunias. Further up the hillside, a *potager,* a kitchen garden of tomato plants, aubergines, melons, and a strawberry patch had started pushing up. Near the entrance gate, hollyhocks waved against a wall of pines. White butterflies darted among sprigs of lavender covering the slopes. With the flowers, the songbirds returned. At dawn thrushes trolled, and after dark a watch of nightingales echoed in the woodlands, an obbligato to the rubbed-leg song of cicadas.

Inside, La Sérafine was as beautiful as outside. Madame Verdeau had at last found us a strong and willing Italian woman anxious to polish the tiles and wax the wood. All we had to do was unpack and live in the house. I didn't mind how many friends came to visit. At last, we were prepared for them. La Sérafine had reached the stature of an ark afloat in a sea of vineyards, an escape to reality and the center of a special and delicious way of life.

Now everyone comes. Beau-Père, at first the sworn enemy of La Sérafine, has become its most faithful client. No sooner do we announce our arrival than he is on the next all-night train across France to join us. Jacques and Nicole and my American family spend vacations with us, the nationalities and generations living in peaceful coexistence. When Beau-Père asserts his tribal authority over the clan, his tyranny is met more with *tendresse* than contempt by the young. A measure of filial piety still holds in France and Jacques and Nicole listen with tolerance, if not abject acquiescence, to their grandfather. They both love La Sérafine and they accept being *en famille* as the human condition. No one is excluded, and age comes before beauty. When Beau-Père prates at them about the rebellion of the new generation, they tease him by calling his violin a *crincrin,* a squawk box, and, remind him jokingly that he eats and drinks for ten, far more than they do.

Il est formidable, they admit, and indeed Beau-Père, the patriarch, is a wonder of vigor and vitality. His spirit vibrates through his deep persuasive voice; his dark, demonic eyes mesmerize; and though he is smaller and more meager than ever, his unquenchable appetite, if anything, increases. A marathon walker as well as a nonstop talker, he scampers up and down the hillside, covering ten kilometers a day, dropping in on all the neighbors. In a village of characters such as Séguret, he is the outstanding character. As a musician and a voracious reader well versed in politics, he commands not the usual tolerance accorded *un vieux monsieur,* but a respect bordering on reverence. Everyone recognizes him with his flowing white hair and silver-knobbed cane as he strides down the road. I suspect he is campaigning, as there is talk of Paul-Marc's being elected mayor of Séguret.

Even if only a rumor, the possibility of his being considered for electoral office proves how deeply we have become involved in the life of Séguret. We are accepted by the villagers as part of their world, members of the wine cooperative, farmers who work the land, contributors to the community group, *les amis de Séguret.* And through us and our stream of international visitors, Séguret, once a sleepy unknown hamlet, has gained a far-flung reputation as an oasis of peace and beauty. But we have not changed, nor could we, the basic rhythm of life of our village. If anything, it has changed us, and when we are in Séguret, we live as the Séguretiens. Here, when the world seems on the verge of falling apart, the center holds.

When I walk under the apricot trees by the pool and look up at the strong white house on the hill, I am filled with wonder and respect for all the people who helped us transform our pile of stones from an abandoned, unpromising peasants' *mas* into *la maison blanche,* as it is called by the people in the plain.

Our house is still by no means finished, nor do we want it to be. There are always new ideas for the rooms, improvements for the park, an expansion of the orchards. Monsieur Verdeau is clearing a terrace for a hundred more cherry trees and putting in an alley of plane trees, the *platanes* of Provence, along the lane to the pool. He found me an old-fashioned yellow *charrette à foin,* a high-wheeled hayrack now outmoded by tractors, to use as a barbecue wagon. Our graveled courtyard is being paved in Provençal tiles by Robert Charrasse. Monsieur Aymard is carving a solid-oak portal to replace the glass-paneled door at the west entrance and Monsieur Bonell will install central heating. La Sérafine must stretch and grow, reaching beyond its pattern as a summer place to become our house for all seasons. One day, irrevocably, the situation will be reversed. We will visit New York and Paris, and live at La Sérafine, not just for a week of grape harvesting or a month of holidays, but for years. By then, La Sérafine will be a microcosm, with our trees bearing fruit, our garden growing food, our cellars full of wine.

Last summer, Beau-Père suggested that we buy a family plot in the secluded, cypress-spired graveyard of Séguret, which perches on a cliff above the full expanse of God's Plain.

"Why?" asked Paul-Marc incredulously. "This is the place where we want to *live.*"

"But, mes chers enfants," he replied, "can you think of a more beautiful place to die?"

A NOTE ON THE TYPE

The text of this book was set on the Linotype in Fairfield, a type face designed by the distinguished American artist and engraver Rudolph Ruzicka. This type displays the sober and sane qualities of a master craftsman whose talent has long been dedicated to clarity. Rudolph Ruzicka was born in Bohemia in 1883 and came to America in 1894. He has designed and illustrated many books and has created a considerable list of individual prints in a variety of techniques.

This book was composed, printed, and bound by The Colonial Press, Inc., Clinton, Massachusetts. Typography and binding design by Anthea Lingeman. Drawings by Fritz Kredel.

Printed in the United States
1387700002B/7-9

9 780595 091652